YOU'D BETTER BELIEVE THIS TOO!

Bible-based resources for youth groups

Ten further sessions on doctrine for 13-18 year olds

Written by Steve Tilley

CONTENTS

YOU'D BETTER BELIEVE THIS TOO!

WHAT'S IT ALL ABOUT?
This book is a companion to *You'd Better Believe It!* in which we looked at ten basic Christian doctrines.* Here are ten more.

As Christians we need to use our Bibles to identify the key Christian doctrines and do our best to understand them. This book can only be seen as a 'starter kit'. Many theologians have devoted their whole lives to polishing the precious stone of Christian doctrine into a beautiful jewel. The reality of understanding doctrine is, sadly, hard work and dedication.

We hope that as you study these key doctrines with your group, the members will be excited by the idea of getting to grips with theology and will have their eyes opened to the possibility of further study.

WHAT'S IN IT?

How to Use This Book	Page 3
Useful Books	Page 5
Teaching Doctrine to Your Group	Page 6
Working in a Non-book Culture	Page 7
Doctrine-conscious Ice-breakers	Page 9

Session 1	THE BIBLE	A Word for All Reasons	Page 11
Session 2	GOD THE FATHER	Father Figures	Page 16
Session 3	JESUS' DIVINITY	Oh My God!	Page 21
Session 4	JESUS' HUMANITY	Who Man Jesus?	Page 26
Session 5	JESUS' ASCENSION	Going Up	Page 31
Session 6	THE TRINITY	Threedom	Page 36
Session 7	THE PERSON OF THE HOLY SPIRIT	Up Close and Personal	Page 41
Session 8	THE WORK OF THE HOLY SPIRIT	Danger – Spirit at Work!	Page 46
Session 9	THE CHURCH AS BODY	Body Language	Page 51
Session 10	THE CHURCH AS FELLOWSHIP	Getting Churched	Page 56

Puzzle solution	Page 61
About CYFA/Pathfinders	Page 62
About Covies	Page 63
Other resources from CPAS / Covies	Page 64

---

* The topics in You'd Better Believe It! are

Who Am I?	The Cross – Cross-words
God – Holy, Sovereign, Creator	The Resurrection – Tomb with a View
God – Loving, Caring, Acting	The Second Coming – Ready or Not?
Sin – The Heart of the Matter	Judgement – Guilty or Not Guilty?
Sin – Truth Decay	Heaven and Hell – Final Destinations

How to Use This Book

With a hey and a ho and a hey nonny no (how do you spell 'nonny no'?), it's that awkward 'How To Use This Book' page. *You'd Better Believe This Too!* is designed to help you (the youth leader) teach the Bible (a book that contains all things necessary for salvation) to your group (that lot over there). There are a number of ways you could go about it.

You could, for instance, read this book through and then do all the interesting games and activities in a row. Might be fun, that, but it wouldn't actually teach anything, except possibly, fun. Then again, you could read the book through from beginning to end and use the material to adapt a teaching programme that will be perfect for your group's age, academic ability and Christian commitment.

On the off-chance that you are neither so daft as to do the former, nor so endowed with time as to do the latter, here's a cunning plan.

The cunning plan

1. Speed-read the book. Get the idea, the big picture, the flavour (sort of strawberryish we reckon).

2. Plan how it might fit into your teaching programme without doing all ten sessions consecutively. Go for three or four in a row and then take a break for something lighter. It is also possible that you may have covered some of the subjects in *You'd Better Believe This Too!* quite recently. Leave them out. We're not proud. We recommend grouping the three sessions on Jesus; likewise the two on the Holy Spirit and the two on the Church.

3. As you approach the material, be sure to read two or three weeks ahead. Some activities require preparation more than a few hours in advance. There are also some suggested peripheral activities (films to watch, surveys to do, guests to invite) that either take a whole session by themselves or require you to give a few weeks' or days' notice.

4. Prepare each session by choosing material. There is too much in each one for a 'normal' group. (If you have a 'normal' group please tell us about it; we've never met one.)

The code We've used this pretty bloomin' clever code throughout.

✪ ✪ ✪ *Essential* As a guide, these sections provide enough material for approximately half an hour's teaching.

✪ ✪ *Desirable* Good supplementary material to take your session up to about an hour.

✪ *Additional* Extra material for longer meetings or to provide variety for groups of different age or ability. Includes activities of a lighter nature. Select and

HOW TO USE THIS BOOK

adapt. Take longer than one session over one session, if you want. You're the boss.

The sessions Each session of *You'd Better Believe This Too!* is divided into:
- ◆ **Teaching Point**
- ◆ **Group Aim**
- ✎ **Equipment Checklist**
- ☞ **Leaders' Guide**
- ☞ **Bible Background**
- ➤ **Starting It, Teaching It and Doing It – The main teaching content.**
- ✍ **Work-out – copyright-free, photocopiable pages for members.**

And almost finally… Pray through the content and pray for the members of your group.

Read the passage, and any appropriate commentaries, thoroughly.

NOT SEX, BUT…

Relationships Sorry about the heading; wanted you to read on, you see. Relationships are crucial. People are important. Share your life with them and they will learn about the Christian life from being with you. Mr Wise (Mark Ashton actually) said: '…the drive home in the car afterwards will again authenticate the message of the Bible study. Does our driving show real respect for authority?' (*Christian Youth Work*, Monarch). As youth leaders we need to lead consistent Christian lives. Otherwise it is like teaching our children to eat their greens whilst focusing our own diets on burgers and fries.

Some good news Many books of this type require you to buy enough copies for every member to have one, or at minimum, every leader. We reckon that you only have to buy one copy per group as any members' material is photocopiable. Multiple copies are only really necessary if you have multiple leaders and don't want to keep passing the books backward and forward. If there's another group nearby, why not do a deal with them to buy other books from CYFA / Covies and swap when you've finished with them.

And finally We've enjoyed preparing this material. CYFA and Covies produce two new books like this every year. We love feedback. Tell us what worked and what didn't. Tell us anything that will help us to write more usefully in future. If you've written stuff to use with your group, why not tell us about it?

Enjoy.

Useful Books

The following books are referred to in the text of *You'd Better Believe This Too!* They may not all still be available, but here are details of the publishers. CPAS Sales carry materials from many other Christian publishers too. If you do not have a catalogue do phone and ask for one. It will cost you nothing (but you'll probably want to buy loads of the amazing resources once you've read it).

The Dramatised Bible, Marshall Pickering

The Ichthus File (Bible Study Notes), St Matthias Press

The Illustrated Bible Dictionary, IVP

Disciple's Study Bible, New International Version, Holman Bible Publishers, Nashville

Jesus For A New Generation, Kevin Ford, Hodder and Stoughton

The Man They Crucified, R. T. France, IVP (currently out of print)

It Makes Sense, Stephen Gaukroger, Scripture Union

Discovering Prayer, Andrew Knowles, Lion

Doctrine Matters, Gordon Kuhrt (Editor), Hodder and Stoughton (currently out of print)

The Origins of New Testament Christology, I. H. Marshall, IVP

Know The Truth, Bruce Milne, IVP

Jesus: The Fact Behind The Faith, C. Leslie Mitton, A. R. Mowbray (currently out of print)

The Message, Eugene H. Peterson, Scripture Press

Why Nobody Learns Much of Anything at Church and How to Fix It, Thom and Joani Schultz, Group

Reflected Glory, Tom Smail, Hodder and Stoughton (currently out of print)

Teaching Doctrine to Your Group

Doctrine. Yuk! What a horrible word. Sounds either severely surgical or thoroughly theological. I think I'll steer clear.

But wait. Just because people use expressions like 'systematic theology' or 'apologetics' it doesn't mean everyone has to talk like that. When we talk about doctrine we are talking about what Christians believe – and why.

Many of the members of your group will have experienced being quizzed by their friends about their faith. Sound Christian doctrine will equip them to answer some of the more difficult questions:

> How can Jesus be wholly God and wholly man?
>
> What is the Holy Spirit?
>
> Do you have to go to church to be a Christian?

These, and many other questions, get the CYFA / Covies treatment in *You'd Better Believe This Too!*

Equipped — So, teaching doctrine to your group will equip young people to live as Christians in their home, family, neighbourhood, school/work and church. It will also give them enquiring minds, anxious to understand. Down the ages the church has been indebted to such thinkers and many steps forward in theology have been made because Christians were not content simply to be told doctrines; they wanted to work them out for themselves from the Bible and understand them.

Exploration — Theology is a developing art. We have our Bibles as the key resource, but many of the great affirmations of the Apostles' Creed were worked out by councils of the church over several centuries. There have never been any easy proof-texts to back up our understanding of, for instance, the Trinity.

So encourage young people to get stuck into their exploration.

Active learning — Then there is that second awkward word – teaching. As leaders of youth groups we need to try and grasp the best educational methods. School has moved on from chalk and talk. A long way on. Our sessions are littered with active-learning methods. Members will understand because in *You'd Better Believe This Too!* they are involved in a process of working things out for themselves. This book does not contain a single lecture. Where there is input, it's in short bursts and there are suggested illustrations.

Teaching doctrine – not so boring as it sounds.

Working in a Non-Book Culture

Non-book culture. *What that then?*

Well, it doesn't mean 'illiterate culture'. Non-book people can, in the main, read, but choose not to read books. Statistics (non-maths people can switch off for a bit here) are varied, but it is alleged that 60 per cent of the population of Great Britain reads one book a year or less.

Increasingly, people are accessing information visually (but from screens rather than print) or aurally. Members of our groups will probably (but not inevitably) be happier with video or CD than with books. They may well read magazines, and some magazines run to over 200 pages these days, but these may demand less concentration and can be taken in bite-sized chunks.

Open book How can you, the youth leader, make the material in *You'd Better Believe This Too!* accessible to non-book groups?

The first, and most obvious thing to say is that we are teaching the Bible and the Bible is a book. Don't put members off if they can't handle a book of 1000 plus pages. How about:

- Getting the passages or verses you are studying typed out onto a single sheet.
- Putting the passages onto acetate and displaying them on OHP.
- Reading aloud the passages yourself. For 1500 years after Jesus' death and resurrection the Bible was communicated in this way.
- Using active learning methods.

Active approach Active learning takes more preparation but will enable people to retain more information. It is biblical. Most of life is an active learning programme.

Sometimes this is described as an ancient Chinese proverb:

> I hear and I forget;
> I see and I remember;
> I do and I understand.

It may well be ancient, but then again it may have been a recent saying to which the author wanted to add weight. Either way, it's true. Learning by activity helps memory and understanding.

WORKING IN A NON-BOOK CULTURE

EXERCISE 1:
A LITTLE LEARNING

Ask members (or leaders in your team meeting if you have one) to write down all the ways of learning they can think of. Write each onto an index card. Shuffle the cards and deal them out. Ask the group to place the cards in a line on the floor, where one end represents 'effective' and another 'ineffective'. Try doing it again with one end representing 'found in the Bible' and the other 'not found in the Bible'.

Discuss the preferred ways of learning and then review your past programme with this in mind.

EXERCISE 2:
SENSE APPEAL

Has your recent teaching appealed to all the different senses (sight, hearing, taste, touch, smell)?

Imagine that you have to use one of the sessions in this book and develop the activities so that all the senses are being bombarded, not just the ears. How will you do it?

Opportunists welcome

So, to summarize: • Use activity.   • Appeal to all the senses.

Best of all, be the sort of person who uses opportunities to teach or lead exploratory learning, when the time is right. A discussion on forgiveness and revenge will go much better the day after one of your members has been beaten up at school than on the day before. Teaching on correct Trinitarian doctrine will be appropriate if the Jehovah's Witnesses have recently been active in the area and some of your members have been doorstepped.

EXERCISE 3:
CHECK YOUR INPUT

The only way to find out about your group's reading culture is to ask them. Do a survey (not a written one). Get them all to shut their eyes (eliminating peer pressure) and ask them questions about their reading habits.

For each of the ten questions give the following choice of answers:
None   1-5   5+

In the last month:
How many books have you read?
How many videos have you watched?
How many magazines have you read?
How many letters have you written?
How many CDs have you bought?
How many times have you been to the cinema?
How many conversations have you had that lasted longer than thirty minutes?
How many essays have you written?
How many sermons have you enjoyed?
Your own, locally relevant, question.

Reading matters

Finally, don't be content with the lack of book skills in your group. The Christians of the eighteenth century were so angry about the lack of reading ability in their churches that they started Sunday Schools. The original Sunday School movement (Gloucester, 1780) started in order to help poorly educated Christians to read so they could get to know the Bible for themselves.

Just occasionally, try some things that require book skills. They may provide just the incentive your young people need to have a go at reading the Bible. Beware of any feelings of smugness in assuming that your group is 'non-book culture'. They may be more interested in reading than they think.

Doctrine-conscious Ice-breakers

Sometimes it is difficult to dive straight into the ice-cold waters of teaching doctrine. You need to break the ice before you can swim. One or more of these games may thaw things out a little....

1. Flour pie
LINK! Getting doctrine correct keeps us clean and saves us from falling.

How old is this game? Place a coin in the bottom of a mixing bowl. Compress flour into the bowl. Invert the bowl onto a tray so the coin now sits on top of the moulded flour. Remove the bowl. Participants take it in turns to cut through the flour, from top to bottom, with a knife. The aim is to make a clean cut without disturbing the coin. The unfortunate victim who causes the coin to fall has to get the coin out of the flour with their teeth. Have a cloth handy.

2. Table-footie
LINK! The Trinity. Strength is in threes. Three in one.

In a hall, or outdoors on a field, play human table-football. Members separate into two teams and each team divides into threes. (If numbers are not divisible by three, have a system of substitutions.)

Players link elbows with their two colleagues and then hold their left and right hands together behind their backs. These 'threes' take up a position on the pitch as in a bar table-football game. They must not release hands or break the links and can move only from left to right, not back and forth.

Introduce the ball. Play.

3. Disguises
LINK! Church consists of individuals. We're all different.

Cut out some well-known faces from a newspaper or magazine. Then disguise them with beards, moustaches, sunglasses, hats, masks, etc. Members have a few minutes to work out who's who.

4. Best invention
LINK! Think how the world has changed since Christian doctrine first began to be formulated in the early centuries AD.

In a recent survey, the flush-toilet was voted the invention which has most improved the life of modern society. Take your own survey. Which invention of the last 2000 years do your members most appreciate?

5. Pairs
LINK! The Bible and Christian doctrine are a necessary match too.

Place a pack of playing cards face-down on the ground. Turning over two cards, one at a time, members try and find a matching pair. If they succeed they keep the pair and get another turn. If they fail they return the cards to the place they found them.

The winner is the person with the most cards when all have been taken.

DOCTRINE-CONSCIOUS ICE-BREAKERS

6. Interruptions
LINK! Encourage questions. 'I teach' does not mean 'you learn'.

This exercise will help you more than the members, but it has an important lesson for them too. Explain that you are going to tell a well-known story but that you want to encourage interruptions. (You may have to prime one or two people to start things off.)

Imagine you are going to tell the story of Snow White. After saying, 'Once upon a time...' someone shouts out, 'When exactly? We need to know?' The dialogue might continue:

'In a land far away...'
Where? Is it still there? What's it called?
'...there lived a beautiful girl called Snow White...'
Why was she called that? Did she have leprosy? What is beauty anyway?
'...and in that land there lived a wicked Queen...'
What do you mean wicked? Was she wicked good, or wicked bad?

7. New facts
LINK! Fellowship. Togetherness. Building up the common life.

Encourage members to spend five minutes talking to each other and to find out one thing they did not know about as many others as they can. The person with the most introduces their new-found facts to everyone else.

8. Truth and lies
LINK! The important thing about Christian doctrine is that it is the truth.

Ask one or two members to tell a story of a time when they were lied to (not by another member but by someone outside the group). Ask how they felt and what they did.

Talk about lies that the world tells, such as:
'Money can buy you happiness.'
'These clothes will make you look more attractive.'
'It doesn't matter what you believe as long as you are sincere.'

9. Evangelism
LINK! Sounds doctrine equals sound evangelism.

Evangelist Arthur converts 50,000 people a year. Evangelist Brenda converts one a year, but so thoroughly and soundly that each of her converts goes on to convert and disciple one person per year – and the converts' converts continue the pattern. Who will achieve 1,000,000 converts first?

Answer After twenty years Arthur will reach one million, with Brenda lagging behind at 524,288. However, Brenda will close the gap the following year. After that she and her converts will go doubling off into the sunset.

10. Teaching
LINK! Doctrine isn't facts taught in a vacuum. It is related to everyday life. It is useful.

Sit everyone in rows. Make them listen.
Read out a succession of at least twenty unrelated, trivial facts.

Hand out pencils and paper. Have a test to see who can remember the most.

EQUIPMENT CHECKLIST
(Depending on which sections you tackle, you may need)
- A supply of blindfolds
- Flip-chart or overhead projector
- Appropriate pens
- Bibles
- Visual aids
- Copies of the *Book of Common Prayer*
- Paper and pens for members
- Copies of Work-out sheet
- Bookmark prize

SESSION 1: THE BIBLE

A Word for All Reasons

◆ TEACHING POINT
The Bible contains all that we need in order to be saved.

◆ GROUP AIM
For members to understand that they need rely on no other source for guidance.

☞ **LEADERS' GUIDE**

It is said that teenagers today are looking for things that work. It is more important that something works than that it is true, they say. This goes some way towards explaining drug and alcohol use. In the short term they give a buzz. They seem to work.

In this session you need to demonstrate that using the Bible is important because it works and because it is true. Most people who try drugs or alcohol don't do so because it is sensible. They do so because they think they are going to work. Be prepared to do battle with any suggestion that the Bible is not worth trying. Rather, encourage the attitude that members should, 'Taste and see that the Lord is good' (**Psalm 34:8**). Drug users soon find that they are addicted to falsehood; a short-term high leads to a long-term lie. Bible users find they are addicted to truth.

☞ **BIBLE BACKGROUND**

Scripture is God's word (**Psalm 78:1-6**). It is inspired by God (**I Thessalonians 1:5,6**) and it communicates God's purpose (**Deuteronomy 17:18-20**). It came to us through a process of writing down (**1 Peter 5:12**), collection (**Colossians 4:16**) and canonization (**2 Peter 3:15-16**).

You will find many verses to illustrate each of these points. We have given just one example of each.

➤ STARTING IT

Hiding
⭐ ⭐

Start the meeting with all the Bibles locked or hidden away. Ask what difference it would make if we no longer had any Bibles. Brainstorm answers onto a flip-chart or overhead projector. Try a subsidiary question, 'What if we had never had any Bibles?' Find them by playing hide-and-seek if your group will enjoy it.

Survey in the dark
⭐ ⭐ ⭐

If you ask your members to raise a hand in order to indicate their opinion, inevitably they will look around at each other before responding. Cancel out

SESSION 1

this peer pressure by doing the survey in the dark. If you trust them, ask them to close their eyes as they answer. If you don't trust them, then get them to blindfold each other first.

So, ask them to raise a hand if they:

1. Have a Bible of their own.
2. Read the Bible and pray by themselves every day.
3. Manage every other day.
4. Read the Bible but don't pray.
5. Pray, but don't read the Bible.
6. Have read the Bible from cover to cover.
7. Have read the New Testament.
8. Have read a Gospel (explain that this means Matthew, Mark, Luke or John).
9. Think the Bible is boring.
10. Want to try to get to know the Bible better.

All these questions provide you with useful information, but the last question is the key one. If your group want to get to know the Bible better then you do not need to spend so much time on learning why the Bible is important. You can major on its content. If more than a few members don't want to get to know the Bible better then you need to focus your teaching in this session on why we should read the Bible.

Indispensable

Prepare a number of visual aids of items with bits missing. Examples would be cars without wheels or racketless tennis players. You could produce a lock and no key, or a pen with no ink. Introduce the session by explaining that you are going to be dealing with the importance of the Bible. It is as essential to a Christian as wheels are to a car.....

➤ TEACHING IT

Article 6

The basis of faith of the Church of England is set out in the Thirty-nine Articles of Religion. Article Six begins: 'Holy Scripture containeth all things necessary to salvation: so that whatsoever is not read therein, nor may be proved thereby, is not to be required of any man, that it should be believed as an article of the Faith, or be thought requisite or necessary to salvation....'

Now you could put that in your pipe and smoke it but how about doing this? Read the statement out quickly. Then give members, perhaps working in pairs, two minutes to write out their version in modern language.

Alternatively have copies of the *Book of Common Prayer* available and see how long it takes members to find Article 6. Then do the exercise.

Happening

Send most members out of the room. Get at least one reliable member to remain. (You don't have reliable members? Try some trust exercises.) Arrange for something to happen for a minute or so. It needs to be something that those remaining can watch. Perhaps a leader can come out to the front and do a series of actions such as:

SESSION 1

1. Take out pen.
2. Unscrew cap.
3. Take paper out of pocket.
4. Unfold it carefully.
5. Write a couple of sentences.
6. Put pen back in pocket.
7. Fold up paper.
8. Take envelope out of pocket.
9. Put paper in envelope.
10. Seal.
11. Mime forgetfulness.
12. Unseal envelope.
13. Take out letter.
14. Write something else.
15. Refold and seal.
16. Put envelope and pen back in pocket.

Get the reliable member to write a detailed account of precisely what happened. Invite one of the 'outsiders' back into the room and get everyone else to explain what happened. Ask that person to explain to one of the others who wasn't there. Continue for as long as you have members outside.

Finally, read the written account to the last member and compare it with the verbal account given by the second and third-hand witnesses. Underline the fact that God has arranged for the important truths of our faith to be recorded by reliable witnesses. Read **John 20:30-31**.

A talk ★★★

In *It Makes Sense* (Scripture Union), Stephen Gaukroger makes these five key points about the Bible. Use them to structure a short talk.

A Message From God To Be Trusted?

Introduction You can't prove, scientifically, that the Bible is God's word. It won't change the colour of litmus paper or do anything else that 'proves' in that way. But you can produce evidence that would convince a court. This law-court model of proof involves listening to the evidence and reaching a verdict. Here are five points that make the case that the Bible is reliable.

1. Manuscripts The Bible contains many eye-witness accounts written by reliable scribes a short time after the events that were being described. Read **1 Corinthians 15:6**. Paul invites his readers to believe the resurrection on the testimony of witnesses who were still alive at the time he wrote.

2. Archaeology Although the Bible is not supported 100 per cent by archaeology, time and again evidence has emerged that points to the reliability of Scripture. The walls of Jericho did fall down (**Joshua 6**) but the ruins of Ai (**Joshua 8**) have proved harder to locate. There was a pool at Bethesda (**John 5**) although for years experts couldn't find it. Archaeology doesn't disprove the Bible and each archaeological advance seems to add weight to the accuracy of Scripture.

3. Prophecy The prophecies in the Bible have come true. Read extracts from **Isaiah 52:13 - 53:12**. This was written centuries before Jesus' birth. It is a remarkably accurate description of his death.

SESSION 1

4. Survival In pure Darwinian terms, the Bible is a proven survivor. All the things thrown at it over the years from atheists, liberal theologians and even government bans, have not dented its popularity. It is still bought, translated into new languages and made the centre of people's lives.

5. It works! Well we think it does anyway or we wouldn't be writing this stuff. The Bible is a guidebook through life. It is 'a lamp to my feet and a light for my path' (**Psalm 119:105**). The Bible is God's backing track for our lives and we need to listen to it and try to sing in tune.

Canonization

Explain that much of the Bible consists of letters or history. Give out the Work-out sheet. Ask members to write down what bits of writing they would assemble into a collection of today's wisdom. The list could include plays, poems, history and letters. Let them compare notes after a few minutes. Explain that listing and trying to agree is the first part of the process of canonization.

Point out the true canon as listed on the Work-out sheet. Explain about the Apocrypha: we may gain examples of life and behaviour from it, but cannot use its books to establish doctrine.

➤ DOING IT

Bibles and notes

This would be a good time to show members how many different versions of the Bible there are. You could do this as a quiz, using the following initials, and getting them to guess the answer. Prize of something appropriate (bookmark?) for the winner.

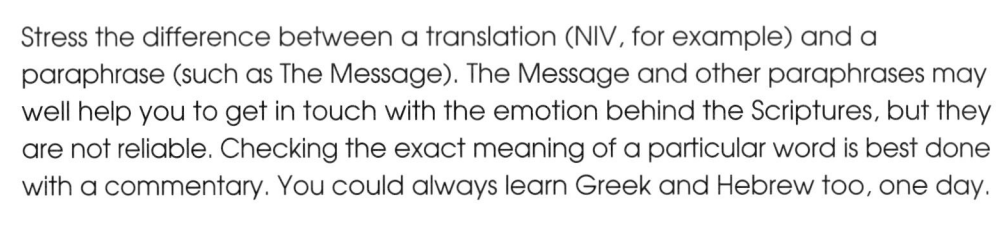

Stress the difference between a translation (NIV, for example) and a paraphrase (such as The Message). The Message and other paraphrases may well help you to get in touch with the emotion behind the Scriptures, but they are not reliable. Checking the exact meaning of a particular word is best done with a commentary. You could always learn Greek and Hebrew too, one day.

GNB	The Good News Bible	TM	The Message
TEV	Today's English Version		(by Eugene Peterson)
RSV	The Revised Standard Version	TYB	The Youth Bible
NEB	The New English Bible	JBP	J.B. Phillips' translation
AV	The Authorised Version	JB	The Jerusalem Bible
KJB	The King James' Bible	DB	The Dramatised Bible
LB	The Living Bible	NIV	The New International Version

Finish by showing people a selection of Bible-reading notes which you should be able to borrow from your local Christian bookshop on sale or return. Please make sure you include the excellent Ichthus File (St Matthias Press).

Memory verse

If you want one, go for **Psalm 119:105**.

PAGE 14

THE CANONIZATION PROCESS WHICH SCRIPTURE HAS GIVEN US...

Testament	Type of Writing	General Name	Specific Name
Old	History and Law	The Pentateuch	Genesis
			Exodus
			Leviticus
			Numbers
			Deuteronomy
	History	History	Joshua
			Judges
			Ruth
			Samuel
			Kings
			Chronicles
			Ezra
			Nehemiah
			Esther
	Drama, Poetry and Proverbs	Wisdom	Job
			Psalms
			Proverbs
			Ecclesiastes
			Song of Solomon
			Lamentations
	Prophecy	The Major Prophets	Isaiah
			Jeremiah
			Ezekiel
			Daniel
	Prophecy	The Minor Prophets	Hosea
			Joel
			Amos
			Obadiah
			Jonah
			Micah
			Nahum
			Habakkuk
			Zephaniah
			Haggai
			Zechariah
			Malachi

Testament	Type of Writing	General Name	Specific Name
New	Biography, History	Gospels	Matthew
			Mark
			Luke
			John
			Acts
	Letters		Romans
			Corinthians
			Galatians
			Ephesians
			Philippians
			Colossians
			Thessalonians
			Timothy
			Philemon
			Hebrews
			James
			Peter
			John
			Jude
	Apocalyptic		Revelation
Apocrypha			Esdras
			Tobias
			Judith
			Wisdom
			Esther Part 2
			Sirach,
			Baruch
			Three Children
			Susanna
			Bel
			Manasses
			Maccabees

If I was 'canonizing' today and had no Bible to draw on I would use ....
....
....
....

WORK-OUT

EQUIPMENT CHECKLIST
(Depending on which sections you tackle, you may need)
- Pens and index cards
- Prepared index cards
- Abba songs
- Video of a soap
- Bibles, or typed-out copies of **Luke 15:11-32**
- Flip-chart or OHP and pens
- Prepared quote on acetate or flip-chart
- Wallpaper
- Glossy magazines
- Scissors, glue
- Words and music for songs

SESSION 2: GOD THE FATHER

Father Figures

◆ TEACHING POINT
God's relationship with us as his people is best understood in terms of father and child.

◆ GROUP AIM
That members would come into that relationship with God as an approachable father rather than a distant figure.

LEADERS' GUIDE

Warning: metaphor alert. God's fatherhood does not directly equate with that of our human fathers. Some members of your group may not have fathers, or may have broken relationships with their fathers.

Jesus referred to himself as 'the good shepherd'. This was to avoid his hearers getting the wrong idea, shepherds being a bunch of ratbags in those days. Bishop James Jones reminds us that we need to make an effort to refer to God as 'the good father', to help those who don't have good experiences of fathers. (Sermon at the Conference of the Group for the Renewal of Worship, Swanwick 1997.)

BIBLE BACKGROUND

Prepare yourself by reading **Hebrews 1:1-9**. In the past God was remote, speaking to most of his people through intermediaries of one sort or another. Now God has revealed himself as Father and speaks through his Son. So we need to look in the Gospels to find out how Jesus, the Son, described the relationship we can have with the one he called 'Abba', Father.

At times of greatest need the word with which Jesus addressed God, the little Aramaic word *abba* (see for instance, **Mark 14:36**), is left untranslated. When he taught the disciples to pray he encouraged them (**Luke 11:2**) to refer to God as Father (Greek: *pater*). We can surmise that an Aramaic *abba* is behind every Greek *pater* we find in the Gospels.

In **Romans 8:15** Paul opens up for us the possibility of our having received a spirit of adoption that enables us, too, to cry 'Abba'.

'When Jesus prayed, he used a word his fellow-Jews would never have dared to use of God. He called him 'Abba' which, in Jesus' mother-tongue, Aramaic, was almost like saying 'Daddy'. It was what Jewish boys and girls called their dads in those days. It was daring, it was shocking – but it summed up the close, intimate relationship he had with God.

'But then he turned to his disciples and taught them to use it too! Not

SESSION 2

everyone can speak of God in this way. Only in the very broadest sense of being God's creatures are we all God's children. But those people whose lives are committed to Jesus can know the same sort of close, deep bond with the God who cares for us in the same way that we care for our youngsters.' (John Balchin, *What Christians Believe*, Lion, 1984.)

This lengthy quote gives us half the picture. It is true, but it is too easy. We do not relate to God as our Father in the same way we relate, ideally, to our fathers today. The 'Abba' relationship in the first-century Jewish community had overtones of lifelong obedience. There are hints of this in the story of the lost son in **Luke 15:11-32**. The expectation was that an obedient son would stay under his father's authority, living and working, until the day the father died. That is why the prodigal's demand for independence goes so much against the grain, and why the 'stay-at-home' son was so resentful of the welcome back his brother received.

➤ STARTING IT

Class Action
⭐

If you want to introduce the theme using a social evening then show a video of the film *Class Action*. This examines the relationship between a father and daughter which is spoiled and then restored.

Abba
⭐

Play some music by Abba as members arrive. What do you mean, 'Who are Abba?'

Father Figure
⭐

Play 'Father Figure' from George Michael's album *Faith*. There are some good images of fatherhood there, but some suggestion that things have gone wrong. Why not write out the lyrics and give a copy to each member and have a brief debate / discussion about the positive and negative aspects of fatherhood in the song.

Missing out
⭐ ⭐ ⭐

Share stories of disappointment. Spend five minutes talking about that cancelled gig, fog-bound cup-tie, missed train or terminated relationship.

You could illustrate this with a short video snatch from one of this week's soap operas where a relationship has gone wrong. (It shouldn't be too hard to find one. *Eastenders* would be a good bet).

Explain that Jesus introduced us to God as our Father so we would not miss out on the best the relationship has to offer.

➤ TEACHING IT

Fatherly feelings
⭐ ⭐ ⭐

Give out pens and index cards. Ask members to write down the first few words that come into their heads when they think of 'father' – one word per

SESSION 2

card. After a few minutes, sort out the cards and see if recurring words suggest any themes. Explain that, when we think of human fatherhood, we have a whole set of pictures in our head, not all of which are appropriate in thinking about God as our Father.

Having said that, swap the cards for some you have prepared earlier with the following words:

Grace	Discipline	Listens
Truth	Punishment	Gifts
Food	Hardship	
Clothes	Forgives	

Get volunteers to read out the following verses, to explain that the words you have substituted are biblical descriptions of God as Father.

John 1:14	Grace, truth
Matthew 6:31	Food, clothes
Hebrews 12:5-8	Discipline, punishment, hardship
Luke 15:21-24	Forgives
Matthew 6:8	Listens
Luke 11:13	Gifts

The lost son

Read the parable of the lost son (**Luke 15:11-32**). Allocate different members to different characters. Very small groups could give more than one character to each member. Very large groups will have more than one member looking at each character. (Why are we telling you this? You're not thick.)

Father (**15:11**)
Younger son (**15:12**)
Older son (**15:12**)
Citizen with pig (**15:15**)
Servant 1 (**15:22**)
Fatted calf – if you must (**15:23**)
Servant 2 (**15:26**)

Read a short section then stop and ask the relevant member how they think their character is feeling at that moment.

Bob Clucas, CYFA Pathfinder Ventures' Trainer, says: 'The parable of the lost son should be retitled, "The Parable of the Two Sons neither of whom Understood the Extent of their Father's Love."' Precisely. Take this remark and put it onto acetate or flip-chart.

Concordance search

Provide a concordance and get members to research all the entries for 'father'. Draw together the interesting ones by writing them on A2 paper or a big piece of wallpaper. Get other members to search through old glossy magazines and cut out images to match the verses.

SESSION 2

➤ DOING IT

Singing
✪ ✪

An appropriate response to God's fatherhood is adoration. Spend some time in praise and thanksgiving to God as your Father. If your group members sing, there are some good, simple, slightly older songs such as:

Hallelujah my Father   God is our Father   Father, we adore you
Abba, Father   Father, we love you

You'll be able to find others in a song book index. Don't fall into the trap of thinking that the only songs worth singing have been written in the last twelve months. (Sorry, that got a bit personal for a moment.)

Our Father
✪ ✪ ✪

Another response to God's fatherhood is to pray. The Lord's Prayer is a delightful example of Jesus approaching God as his Father.

Pray together a modern version of it. Then pray it again, line by line, and allow a time for meditation or open prayer based on each new theme.

Read this short passage aloud to the group:

'We're coming to Almighty God who is also our Father. We aren't phoning through a big order to a department store which sells everything. Nor are we practising some weird and wonderful thought-process guaranteed to release psychic powers. We're coming simply, humbly into the presence of our Creator, having received the invitation to do so from Jesus himself.' Andrew Knowles, *Discovering Prayer*, Lion, 1985.

Memory verse
✪ ✪ ✪

Luke 15:32. '...this brother of yours was dead and is alive again; he was lost and is found.'

Work-out
✪ ✪ ✪

The Work-out sheet is a memory jogger of some of the things we have covered in this session. If you missed out sections then you may need to offer a brief explanation of each quote.

Give members five minutes alone to write out what they want to remember from the session.

WORK-OUT

> 'We need to make an effort to refer to God as, "The good Father", to help those who don't have good experiences of fathers.'
>
> *Bishop James Jones*

> 'We're coming to Almighty God who is also our Father. We aren't phoning through a big order to a department store which sells everything. Nor are we practising some weird and wonderful thought process guaranteed to release psychic powers. We're coming simply, humbly into the presence of our Creator, having received the invitation to do so from Jesus himself.'
>
> *Andrew Knowles, Discovering Prayer, Lion, 1985*

> 'The parable of the lost son should be retitled, "The Parable of the Two Sons neither of whom Understood the Extent of their Father's Love."'
>
> *Bob Clucas, CYFA Venture Leaders' Training Day, 1996*

> 'I will be your father
> I will be your preacher
> I'll be your daddy
> I will be the one who loves you until the end of time.'
>
> *George Michael, 'Father Figure' from* Faith, *Epic 1987*

> '...this brother of yours was dead and is alive again; he was lost and is found'
>
> *Luke 15:32*

When I think of God as my Father I want to remember...

(Invite group members to complete the sentence.)

EQUIPMENT CHECKLIST
(Depending on which sections you tackle, you may need)
- Copies of Work-out sheet
- Three different coloured pens for each member
- OHP and acetate or flip-chart
- Bibles
- Copies of the Gospels
- Visual aids for talk
- A paper bag
- Refreshments

SESSION 3: JESUS' DIVINITY

Oh My God!

◆ TEACHING POINT
Jesus on earth was fully God in human flesh.

◆ GROUP AIM
Through this and the next session, to present Jesus as fully God and fully human – a real, though complex, person.

☞ LEADERS' GUIDE

We're going to do three sessions in a row about Jesus: his divinity, humanity and ascension. To do justice to the subject matter, it really is essential that you cover the first two consecutively. The ideas about Jesus' divinity need to be still in members' minds as you discuss his humanity. This is a complex subject. Theologians have studied for years to arrive at an acceptable explanation of Jesus as fully human and fully divine. No one person can be easily understood as two separate 'fullys'.

To get to grips with this subject we need to jettison some of our preconceptions. We find it hard even to imagine how a person like us can be fully God. But Jesus is not a person 'like us'. He is the ultimate personality – the 'personstick' against whom personality is measured.

We find it equally hard to imagine God, all-powerful, all-knowing, etc., appearing as a human in weakness. This is because our picture of God is too small. A God who willingly chooses self-limitation in order to be with his creation (incarnation) and to save it (salvation) is a bigger God than any of us can imagine.

So, overboard with those presuppositions and hold the two ideas in tension. We're heading into the world of the strange. We're driving right up the middle of Paradox Street here. Two opposite things are going to turn out true at the same time. Prepare for head expansion.

☞ BIBLE BACKGROUND

We cannot prove the Trinity on a scientific model of proof. In fact we cannot do that for any doctrine. The model of proof is that of a court of law. There is evidence and we need to reach a verdict. Here is the evidence:

JESUS WAS GOD IN HUMAN FLESH
Evidence from events and happenings

Virgin birth	**Matthew 1:18**	Wisdom	**1 Corinthians 1:30**
Holy and sinless	**John 8:42-47**	Prophecy	**Micah 5:2**
Miracles	**Mark 1:21-45**	Resurrection	**Mark 16:1-8**
Authority	**Luke 19:45 - 20:8**		

SESSION 3

Evidence from expressions used about him – and by him

'Son of God'	**Matthew 14:33**	'Lord'	**Acts 2:36**
'Son of man'	**Mark 2:10**	'I am'	**John 13:19**
'The Word'	**John 1:1**	'Alpha and Omega'	**Revelation 21:6**

Evidence from God's own affirmation

Baptism	**Mark 1:11**	Transfiguration	**Matthew 17:5**
Resurrection	**Acts 2:24**		

➤ STARTING IT

Read the Gospel ✪ ✪

Why not read through the whole of a Gospel – Mark is a good one because it is the shortest – in one evening? If you choose Mark, take a break at **8:29a** for something refreshing (bread and fish?) and then return to the answer at **8:29b**.

This would need to be done in the week before the session, as a preparation. You could then, perhaps, make sure that the majority of your illustrative material comes from the Gospel you read. Mark will take you about 100 minutes. If you are going to get members to read, make sure they are happy to do so. Give them advance notice so they can practise or ask you about any difficult pronunciations.

Creed ✪ ✪ ✪

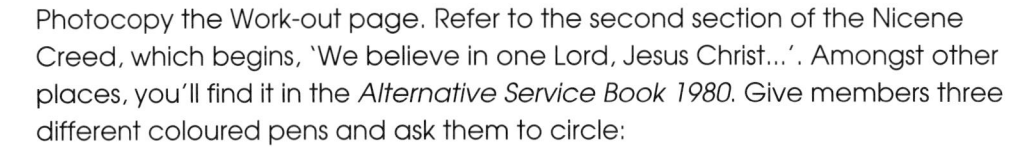

Photocopy the Work-out page. Refer to the second section of the Nicene Creed, which begins, 'We believe in one Lord, Jesus Christ...'. Amongst other places, you'll find it in the *Alternative Service Book 1980*. Give members three different coloured pens and ask them to circle:

Colour 1	Phrases that emphasize Jesus' humanity.
Colour 2	Phrases that emphasize Jesus' divinity.
Colour 3	Phrases they don't fully understand.

It is possible that some bits will have more than one coloured ring.

Teenage Jesus ✪

Draw a line down the middle of the flip-chart paper or acetate to make two columns. Head one column 'Can imagine' and the other 'Can't Imagine'.

Brainstorm traits of teenage behaviour. As each idea is shouted out discuss whether or not you can imagine Jesus doing it.
The key point is that, as a fully divine human being, Jesus was without sin. Therefore if the trait is a sinful one we cannot imagine Jesus doing it, whereas if it is just part of teenage character we can imagine him doing it. Jesus was a real adolescent. In which category does 'Having an untidy room' belong. Is it sinful, or normal?

By the way, untidy rooms are not only the prerogative of teenagers. You should see the author's study when he's in mid-flow..

SESSION 3

➤ TEACHING IT

Titles

✪ ✪ ✪

Working in smaller groups if necessary, give members time to research a Gospel. If you can get hold of some single Gospels in paperback then they would be excellent for this. Ask group members to look through each Gospel for examples of titles of Jesus. Get them to distinguish between titles he used of himself and titles others used of him. Write answers on the Work-out sheet.

In a short input, explain that some of the titles Jesus used of himself seem to have been deliberately vague, e.g. 'Son of man'. We can further our understanding by looking at the titles others gave him, such as the words of his Father at his baptism (**Mark 1:11**) and transfiguration (**Matthew 17:5**). Amazingly, we often find the correct confession of Jesus' divinity on the lips of those from whom he had cast out demons (see **Mark 1:24; 5:7**).

Just another man?

✪ ✪

The short evangelistic talk 'Mad, Bad, Good, God' might be appropriate in this meeting. You need to suggest that there are four possible conclusions about who Jesus is / was.

Mad? No. He was in control. He was as sane as anybody. A man with a mission? Yes. A madman? We don't think so.

Bad? His behaviour of healing, teaching, exorcising, feeding does not tie in with him being bad. If he was a bad man he had amazing compassion.

Good? Well yes. But *only* good? Storm-calming, table-overturning and crucified for blasphemy. There's more to this man than goodness.

God? That leaves us with a heavy conclusion. He was who he said he was: God, made flesh; God, in human form. The Son of the living God, and no less than God himself.

Present these four points, illustrated and visually aided if you can, and then throw it open to question. Read **Mark 8:27-29** and then leave members to answer the question in an open discussion. Give a copy of one of the Gospels to any who haven't read them before.

Beginnings and false ends

✪ ✪

If anything marks out Jesus' divinity it is the way he came into, and didn't go out of, this world.

Divide into two groups, if possible. Get them to refer to the part of the Work-out sheet that asks, 'What's so funny about...?' Get one group to look at **Matthew 1:18-25** and **Luke 1:26-38; 2:1-20**. They should answer the question, 'What's so funny about Jesus' birth?'
The other group should look at **Matthew 27:45 - 28:10; Mark 15:42 - 16:8; Luke 23:44 - 24:12 and John 19:28 - 20:9**. They should answer the question, 'What's so funny about Jesus' death?' If you can find a piece of music with an

PAGE 23

SESSION 3

interesting beginning and a false ending, play it during this activity. (Steve Harley's 'Come Up and See Me' is a good example.)

You can do all of this in one group together, but it will, of course, take longer.

Authorized version ✪

Tell everyone to do something daft. Try these instructions:

Stand up and raise your left hand above your head.
Touch someone else on the right ear with your right hand.
Sit down without letting go.

After the ear surgery is finished, ask them why. Listen to the answers carefully. Explain that they probably did it (if they did) because they are used to you being in charge and they expect there will be a reason for what you tell them. Explain that people had equal difficulties with authority in Jesus' day. Read **Luke 20:1-8** and **Mark 4:41**. Jesus had authority even over the wind and waves, yet it led to confusion over his identity. Some years distant from the events we are forced to the conclusion that his authority was more than God-given; it was actually God-driven – divine authority itself.

B-wise ✪

Ask this question. In a knock-out, singles tennis competition there are 118 entrants. How many matches must there be to decide a winner? Many people will try and solve this with complicated calculations. The wise way to do it is to remember that for there to be one winner there must be 117 losers and therefore 117 matches is the answer. It is lateral thinking. It is human wisdom.

Read **1 Corinthians 1:26-31**. Point out that very shortly after Jesus' resurrection, writers such as Paul were attributing divine wisdom to him. The wise thing to do is put your trust in him. It won't necessarily improve your maths, but it will lengthen your life infinitely.

➤ DOING IT

Applied truth ✪ ✪ ✪

What would change if the whole church took Jesus' divinity seriously? Brainstorm with members and leaders to list as many changes as possible. For instance, a greater reverence in worship when singing about Jesus. Remember that 'At the name of Jesus every knee shall bow', as the hymn goes. Or maybe there should be a greater willingness to serve Jesus because of who he is and what he has already done for us. Resolve that each person in the room will take one of the ideas listed more seriously.

Refreshments ✪ ✪

Offer round some divine refreshments. Go for the best chocolate biscuits you can buy and the finest lemonade. Explain that the truth about Jesus is far more exciting than great food and drink but, unlike what you have provided, it is free. Then issue every member with an extortionate bill for the drinks and food. Tell them you will cancel their debt if they bring the bill with them next time, along with the Work-out sheet.

WORK-OUT

An extract from the Nicene Creed.

We believe in one Lord, Jesus Christ,
the only Son of God,
eternally begotten of the Father,
God from God, Light from Light,
true God from true God,
begotten, not made,
of one Being with the Father.
Through him all things were made.
For us men and for our salvation
he came down from heaven;
by the power of the Holy Spirit
he became incarnate of the Virgin Mary,
and was made man.
For our sake he was crucified under
Pontius Pilate;
he suffered death and was buried.
On the third day he rose again
in accordance with the Scriptures;
he ascended into heaven
and is seated at the right hand of
the Father.
He will come again in glory
to judge the living and the dead,
and his kingdom will have no end.

Titles others used of Jesus...

Titles Jesus used of himself...

What's so funny about...?

FOR NEXT TIME...
Hey, leader person,
I remembered my sheet.
Please cancel my debt.

EQUIPMENT CHECKLIST
(Depending on which sections you tackle, you may need)
- Copy of the song 'Kelly's Heroes' by Black Grape from the album *It's Great When You're Straight Yeah* (Radioactive Records)
- Batman video
- Prepared index cards and two labelled buckets
- Copies of Work-out sheet
- Clipboards and pens
- Song words and musical instruments

SESSION 4: JESUS' HUMANITY

Who Man Jesus?

◆ TEACHING POINT
Jesus was not only fully divine, but also fully human.

◆ GROUP AIM
For the group to draw closer to Jesus because Jesus' full humanity means he can sympathize with our weaknesses.

☞ LEADERS' GUIDE

Jesus' full divinity has to be affirmed. The proper understanding of substitutionary atonement (Jesus died in our place) cannot be maintained if Jesus was just another human being.

'There was no other good enough
To pay the price of sin;
He only could unlock the gate
Of heaven, and let us in.'
('There Is a Green Hill Far Away', C.F. Alexander)

That was the subject of the last session, but is not the end of the story. If Jesus was *only* fully divine, we cannot sing,

'Jesus take me as I am,
I can come no other way.'
(Dave Bryant, Thankyou Music, 1978)

For if he is any less than fully human there is as much a gap between us and Jesus as there is between us and God. How can he then represent us? How can he be our great High Priest? How can he sympathize with our weaknesses? He can still unlock the gates of heaven, but he can't take us inside with him. We're doomed.

At the Council of Chalcedon in 451 AD, statements such as the following were made about Jesus' divinity and humanity:

Two solidarities Jesus Christ is completely one with God and completely one with humanity. True God and true human.

Two origins His divine origin is hidden within the mystery of God, but his human origin has a particular time and place. Mary is his mother.

Two natures The Godhead and the humanity are present in Jesus without the one swallowing up the other. He is neither hybrid nor schizophrenic.

SESSION 4

One person There is one individual. Jesus is not God with a little man inside, nor God in a 'man' costume.

The early councils of the church were acted out with a background of martyrdom for heresy. The cost of getting Christology wrong in the first few centuries after Christ's death and resurrection was very high indeed. We are embarking on a real theological exploration here. You may find it interesting to follow it up yourself for further study. In the meantime the skill is to introduce your members to the complexity of all this without boggling their minds.

☞ BIBLE BACKGROUND

Jesus was a human being led by God's Spirit. He experienced human birth (**Matthew 1:18-25**). He entered into the possibility of human temptation (**Matthew 4:1-11**). He endured human death (**Matthew 27:32-50**).

'...we do not have a high priest who is unable to sympathize with our weaknesses, but we have one who has been tempted in every way, just as we are – yet was without sin. Let us then approach the throne of grace with confidence, so that we may receive mercy and find grace to help us in our time of need' (**Hebrews 4:15,16**).

To have a balanced view of Jesus' humanity / divinity we need to go to a very early New Testament scripture, **Philippians 2:1-11**. For here, Paul has taken what looks like an early Christian hymn and used it to explain the voluntary self-limiting that was going on in God taking flesh, the form of a servant.

As we study it, we will have our view of Jesus' humanity affirmed in every way, yet we will also feel humbled by his example of servant leadership. If we don't feel like washing feet after this session, or even the coffee cups, there is probably no hope for us.

➤ STARTING IT

Remember
✪ ✪

So who remembered last time's Work-out sheet? Cancel their debt. Decide what to do with the ones who forgot – some forfeit or task of service would be appropriate.

Jesus who?
✪

If you can get hold of it, play the song, 'Kelly's Heroes' by Black Grape and discuss the lyrics, especially the memorable:

'Jesus was a black man
Jesus was Batman
No, no, that was Bruce Wayne.'

Many of the songs on Black Grape's album *It's Great When You're Straight Yeah* raise interesting themes. (Warning – occasional choice language!)

SESSION 4

Hiding the humanity
✪ ✪ ✪

Write out on separate index cards a number of 'normal' human activities such as washing, eating, crying, sleeping. Add a few activities that arise out of divinity: for example, healing, exorcising, multiplying food. Hide these cards around the room.

Have two buckets in the centre of the room, one labelled 'divinity' and the other 'humanity'. Send members to search for cards and place them in the appropriate bucket. Debrief by going through the buckets and checking that everyone, including you, agrees.

Do you think Jesus...?
✪

Go round the room taking it in turns to make a statement that begins, 'Do you think Jesus...?' Take a vote each time and discuss any interesting responses. If you're really stuck for examples, how about:

...was any good at carpentry?
...got on with his brothers and sisters?
...liked turnip?
...shaved? (Hmm! Jesus Shaves. It would never catch on as a slogan.)

➤ TEACHING IT

Calling all the heroes
✪ ✪

Give out copies of the Work-out sheet. Working with a partner, get members to devise a comic-book hero. A five-minute video snatch of Batman would not go amiss here. Here's the catch. It has to be a hero with finely-honed, but *earthly*, powers. You can't draw a character with unlikely super-powers (Spiderman, Superman), but only one who has sharpened-up human skills by training and practice.

Jesus was fully human. The only sense in which we can say he had 'super-powers' is that they flowed from his relationship with God the Father.

Who man Jesus?
✪ ✪ ✪

Look at these three Gospel passages in which Jesus' humanity is clearly seen. If you can, divide into three groups and ask each group to research one passage and to list the signs of humanity they see there.

1. His human birth and early years (**Luke 2:1-7, 21, 40, 41-52**).
2. His human temptation (**Matthew 4:1-11**).
3. His human death (**Matthew 27:32-50**).

If any group finishes well before another, give them the additional task of researching further into the Gospels for evidence of Jesus' humanity.

Who do people think he is?
✪

It is good to get your group out in the street doing research every once in a while. They get used to starting 'cold conversations'. This activity will need to be done the week before the meeting.

Go down to a heavily populated area and get members, armed with clip-

PAGE 28

SESSION 4

boards and pens, to ask the question, 'Who do you think Jesus is?' (It's good to phrase it in the present tense rather than the past.) They could do the same survey at their schools too. Record all the answers for use at your meeting.

At the meeting itself, ask members what they expected the public to say and how the actual answers differed. Was there a substantial difference between the answers of school friends and the general public?

Hymn to Christ

Philippians 2:1-11 is set out as the example of imitating Christ's humility, in most Bibles. Use the key section **verses 5-11** to produce a visual aid. You need to draw a huge letter U on the paper or acetate. The top of the U is heaven and the bottom is earth. Members can all copy this as you do it, perhaps on the reverse of the Work-out sheet.

Read through the passage. At each point, mark on the letter U the movement from heaven to earth and back again:

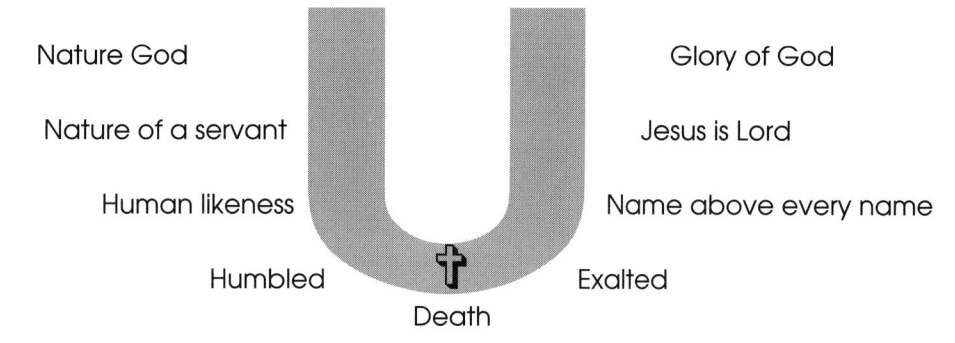

Nature God — Glory of God

Nature of a servant — Jesus is Lord

Human likeness — Name above every name

Humbled — Exalted

Death

Any questions

Check that any questions about Jesus' humanity that are left over from the last session have been dealt with.

▶ DOING IT

Memory verse

'...we do not have a high priest who is unable to sympathize with our weaknesses, but we have one who has been tempted in every way, just as we are – yet was without sin' (**Hebrews 4:15**).

Prayer

In the light of the memory verse you may now like to lead a time of prayer focusing on weaknesses and needs.

Singing

'Lord I Lift Your Name On High' (in most modern song-books) picks up the humanity / divinity question perfectly and echoes the heaven-earth-heaven theme from **Philippians 2**.

Summary

Give members some space to write a summary of what they have learned over the last two sessions, on the Work-out sheet in the two boxes. (You may need to do some prompting / reminding about the previous session.)

WORK-OUT

COMIC-BOOK HEROES
Design your own hero, here:

SUMMARY

1. Jesus' divinity	2. Jesus' humanity

EQUIPMENT CHECKLIST
(Depending on which sections you tackle, you may need)
- Picture of a famous person
- Copies of Work-out sheet
- Pens
- Notebook
- OHP and acetates or flip-chart/ wallpaper and marker pens
- Shoe, T-shirt, sock, pair of shorts, pair of underpants, bra, hat, jumper, umbrella, sunglasses

SESSION 5: JESUS' ASCENSION

Going Up

◆ TEACHING POINT
To teach that Jesus' physical, earthly ministry had an end point.

◆ GROUP AIM
To understand what part Jesus now plays in the life of a believer.

☞ LEADERS' GUIDE

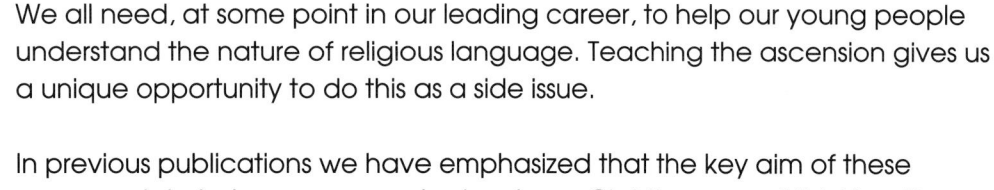

We all need, at some point in our leading career, to help our young people understand the nature of religious language. Teaching the ascension gives us a unique opportunity to do this as a side issue.

In previous publications we have emphasized that the key aim of these resources is to help young people develop a Christian way of thinking. The Bible is so chock-a-block full of picture language, metaphor and time-dated illustrations that we are really failing our groups if we don't help them to understand it in that way.

We need to equip them with the thinking tools to distinguish between historical fact and metaphor. Then they need to understand that not all Christians agree on the answers. Some have even suggested that the resurrection is only an extended metaphor, depicting the good news that God's message couldn't die. Members need to be aware of this.

If you want to read a book that takes a completely different view from that of evangelical Christians, take a look at either *Honest To God* by John A.T. Robinson (SCM, 1963), or the more recent *God In Us* by Anthony Freeman (SCM, 1993).

☞ BIBLE BACKGROUND

Jesus continues to minister for us:

In heaven after his ascension (**Luke 24:50-53; Acts 1:9-12**)
The notes in the *NIV Disciple's Study Bible* are particularly helpful here, so we will quote at length:

'Other Gospels show the gospel could be narrated without the story of the ascension. The resurrection marked Jesus' victory over sin and death, assuring the completion of God's saving acts. The ascension is God's final and confirming act in Jesus. Theologians speak of Jesus' humiliation and his exaltation. The wonders of the virgin birth and the ascension bracket Jesus' earthly existence. The ascension is the only logically possible outcome of God's greatest act in Jesus Christ, the resurrection. The purpose of the ascension was to remove the glorified body of Christ out of earthly, physical

SESSION 5

limitations and to provide the appropriate context for Jesus' homecoming in heaven, God's sphere. There Jesus began his ministry for the church and prepared to return for the final judgement.' (*NIV Disciple's Study Bible*)

Through intercession for us (**Roman 8:31-39**)
Our basis for confidence in prayer today is that Jesus, who has shared human weakness, is at his Father's side. He shares God's authority, but he has an intimate relationship with both God and us (through the Holy Spirit).

Equipping us (**Ephesians 4:7-16**)
The ascended Lord sent back gifts from heaven by the Holy Spirit, equipping us for the day-by-day task of being a Christian.

➤ STARTING IT

Review

Review the memory verse **Hebrews 4:15** (from Session 4). Read **Hebrews 4:14**, then pause for everyone to join in the memory verse (well, we're optimistic about your teaching, OK?), then read **verse 16**.

Explain that this reviews the last session, but also points forward to this one. Jesus has ascended and from his throne is able to help us.

Picture language

Have a picture available of somebody famous. Let's say you choose the Queen. Say, 'That's the Queen!' Brief somebody else to argue, 'No it's not! It's only a picture of Her Majesty!'

The conversation continues:
'Yes I know it's a picture, but it's a picture of the Queen and therefore in a real sense it is the Queen.'
'That doesn't get round the fact that it is not actually her. It is merely a visual representation of her, lovely as it is. It is an icon.'
'But we can talk about the Queen as we look at it. We can discuss her attributes and authority. It takes us into the realm of Queen-ness.'
'But it ain't her.'
'Yes it is.'
'No it isn't.'
'Tis.'
'Tisn't.'
(Fade out)

Throw it open to discussion. Is it the Queen (or whoever you chose) or not?

➤ TEACHING IT

Really real?

Give members, working in small groups if necessary, copies of the Work-out sheet. Ask them to look at

SESSION 5

the passages mentioned and alongside each to note whether they have been reading examples of Luke's picture language or of Luke's factual description. The examples are all taken from in and around the account of the ascension in **Acts 1**.

Acts 1:5	Picture language. Luke describes what receiving the Holy Spirit will be like.
Acts 1:9	Fact. This is what witnesses claim to have seen.
Acts 1:18	Fact. This is what happened to Judas.
Acts 1:26	Fact. This is how the twelfth disciple was chosen.
Acts 2:2,3	Picture language. It was 'like' wind and 'seemed to be' fire.
Acts 2:13	Fact. Luke describes the crowd's reaction.
Acts 2:19,20	Picture language. This is an Old Testament metaphor of the 'last days'.
Acts 2:32	Fact. For Luke, the resurrection is not just a picture, but really true.
Acts 2:37	Picture language. No cutting took place. It is a metaphor.
Acts 2:41	Fact. Luke announces the number of converts, approximately.

Why not? ★ Why did Jesus not stay and minister on earth? Lead into an open discussion. The main reason you are looking for is that as a single, earth-limited human Jesus is only accessible to a few people. Risen and ascended, he is available, by his Spirit, to everybody.

Read the accounts in **Luke 24:50-53** and **Acts 1:9-12**.

What now? ★ Ask members to tell a partner how they felt after something really exciting had finished. Perhaps the moment after the last encore at a great gig, or at the bus-stop after a great match, or when they had finished their last examination. (Never say, 'I've finished my last examination.' You probably haven't.)

In a brief input, suggest that after his birth, life, death, resurrection and ascension you would think Jesus' work was over. This is not what the Bible teaches. We are told that he continues his work, interceding (going-between) for us. Someone who intercedes makes communication possible. Read **Roman 8:31-39**.

You could do the talk by preparing an acetate with the words:

Jesus' birth	Jesus' death	Jesus' ascension
Jesus' life	Jesus' resurrection	Jesus now

Use a piece of paper to slowly reveal each new line as you talk. Even better would be to have six separate acetates, one for each heading – accompanied by an appropriate cartoon.

No OHP? Use a flip-chart or large piece of paper and write each set of words as you get to them with a heavy marker pen. Have a double thickness of

SESSION 5

paper so you don't accidentally write on the wall (spoken from bitter experience).

Kit list

Hide the items mentioned on the Work-out sheet around the room, hall or house – or outdoors in the summer. Members, working in two groups in competition, have to find each item, one at a time. Once found, they have to dress one of their team with the items (over their other clothes – before you ask). Team that gets most items, wins.

Parade the two models and do a brief Venture / camp / houseparty advert. (If you don't understand why then phone Covies Holidays or CYFA Pathfinder Ventures at once and demand an explanation. The numbers are the same as the organizations' main numbers at the back of this book.) Then continue to explain that Jesus' job, post-ascension, is to equip us for ministry. Read **Ephesians 4:7-16**. Say: 'The job description of the ascended Jesus has changed. Salvation is finished. Intercession and equipping is just beginning.'

➤ DOING IT

Vase-filling

The risen, ascended Jesus gives gifts to his people

There are many excellent exercises to help members get in touch with their gifts. We have touched on them in previous publications. Perhaps the best is vase-filling.

Each member writes their name on a piece of paper and draws a container, such as a vase. The pieces of paper are then circulated round the group so every person has a chance to write on everyone else's vase.

The aim is to write down something that you perceive each person to be good at. It is a most encouraging exercise. Nothing negative allowed. When each sheet has been to everybody, take a moment to debrief. Ask members to share if anything is particularly encouraging or surprising.

Don't do this if there are any newcomers who aren't known to other members of the group.

Particularly large groups may have to build some limitations into the exercise, such as working in small groups, or with people members know well. Beware of cliques though.

Intercessions

Use the chance to emphasize the teaching about Jesus interceding for us by having a time of intercessory prayer – that is, asking for things. Why not start recording the things you ask for in a notebook? After a while you can look back at all the answered prayers.

WORK-OUT

REALLY REAL?

Picture language	Historical fact
Acts 1:5	
Acts 1:9	
Acts 1:18	
Acts 1:26	
Acts 2:2,3	
Acts 2:13	
Acts 2:19,20	
Acts 2:32	
Acts 2:37	
Acts 2:41	

KIT LIST

A shoe	A pair of shorts	A bra	An umbrella
A T-shirt	A pair of	A hat	Sunglasses
A sock	underpants	A jumper	

EQUIPMENT CHECKLIST
(Depending on which sections you tackle, you may need)
- Hot drinks, cold drinks and ice lollies
- Bibles
- Copies of Work-out sheet and pencils
- Dressing-up clothes
- Song words/books and musical accompaniment

SESSION 6: THE TRINITY

Threedom

◆ TEACHING POINT
That a proper understanding of our faith must be Trinitarian.

◆ GROUP AIM
For members to be equipped to spot heresy.

☞ LEADERS' GUIDE

I can't resist a brief piece of personal testimony here. I studied Christian doctrine at theological college. The course book for the doctrine of the Trinity was *One God in Trinity*, edited by Toon and Spiceland. In the section on the theology of Karl Barth, contributor Richard Roberts wrote: 'Barth, in positing the contingent historical order upon the basis of the putative contingency and historicity of God, attempts to recreate the natural order but by doing so effects a resolution and extinction of that order in the Trinitarian abyss of the divine being.' I loved that sentence. I read it and read it. I dreamed of the day I might begin to understand what on earth it meant. I'm still dreaming.

Teaching the Trinity to your youth group will not be the easiest thing you have ever done. Managing to make it simple, straightforward and understandable will fly in the face of 2000 years of theological text books.

So don't be overawed. If this session gets your youth group talking about why Christian faith has to be Trinitarian, you will have succeeded. You might even have put into someone's heart the seed-thought that one day they will be able to explain Richard Roberts' sentence to you. Let's go for it.

☞ BIBLE BACKGROUND

The doctrine of the Trinity is a revealed doctrine in the Bible, but cannot be reduced to a proof-text. In order to see the doctrine of the Trinity clearly we must step back from too narrow a view of the Bible (one passage at a time) and see the whole range of scriptural material. Doing this we will see God revealed as One, yet as three individual persons, Father, Son and Holy Spirit. We will see the three appearing separately and also together.

Yet we will also see the deeply monotheistic (*mono*: one; *theos*: God) Old Testament Judaism where the first commandment requires that there be 'no other gods' (**Exodus 20:2,3**). Our biblical material will therefore need to assert that Father, Son and Holy Spirit are all equally divine, separate, yet one. Here's the material:

The Three are separate
Jesus' baptism (**Mark 1:9-11**). Here we have the Son being baptized, accompanied by the voice of the Father and the descent of the Spirit.

SESSION 6

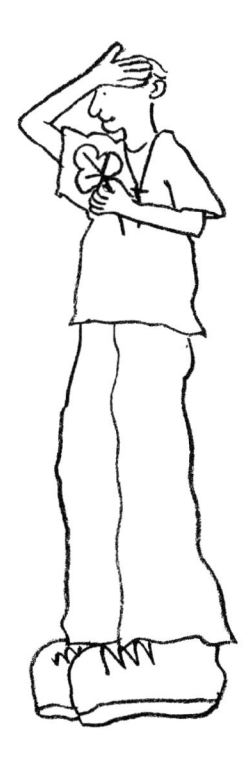

The Three are one
Matthew records Jesus' final words to his disciples, that future converts must be baptized in the name of Father, Son and Holy Spirit (**Matthew 28:19**). Jesus states that he and the Father are one (**John 10:30**).
In addition, although not of itself convincing, the voices of creation are plural (**Genesis 1:26** '...let us make....'; **John 1:1** '...the Word was with God...').

The divinity of the Father
Galatians 1:1. It was the divine command of God, the Father, that raised Jesus from the dead.

The divinity of the Son
Colossians 2:9. All the fullness of God is found in Jesus, in bodily form. See also **Philippians 2:6**.

The divinity of the Holy Spirit
2 Corinthians 3:17. The Spirit is also Lord.

➤ STARTING IT

Drinks

As people arrive, give them a choice of a hot drink, a cold drink or an ice-lolly. As you begin your teaching session, make the point that H2O can appear as ice, water or steam, depending on the temperature. The same chemical formula offers three distinct and different formats. Lead into some introductory remarks about the Trinity and your teaching this session.

Language under pressure

Start with a few tongue-twisters. Try these Scottish football results:

Forfar	4	5	East Fife
East Fife	4	5	Forfar
Cowdenbeath	3	3	Inverness Thistle

Or these:

The sixth sheik's sixth sheep's sick.
Six sticky thumbs.
Flipping frightening for Freda, falling thirty feet.
Make up some more. (That's a suggestion, not a tongue-twister.)

Talking about the Trinity will, inevitably, place our human language under pressure. We can only talk in metaphor and analogy. If you talked about the nature of religious language in your previous session on Jesus' ascension, make the link at this point.

Believe it or what?

Give out copies of the survey on the Work-out sheet. Ask members to answer the questions honestly yet anonymously and then hand them in. Produce a quick bar-chart on paper or acetate to demonstrate the range of answers.

PAGE 37

SESSION 6

Each question will give you a score. You can take an average by dividing the total of the answers by the number of members. Have a calculator handy if your group is large.

This survey will enable you to assess at what level you need to pitch the session. You might, if you don't enjoy thinking on your feet, like to do the survey a whole week in advance.

➤ TEACHING IT

Verse search

Explain that within the pages of the Bible there are many verses that build up a Trinitarian understanding of God, but there is no one proof-text. Give members Bibles and, working in small groups if necessary, ask them to look up the verses on the Work-out sheet. They will have to place the verses in one of the five columns, depending on which part of our understanding of the Trinity the verse contributes to.

The Three are separate
Mark 1:9-11; John 14:16-17a; Acts 2:32-36

The Three are one
Matthew 28:19; John 10:30; Genesis 1:26

The divinity of the Father
Galatians 1:1; Matthew 6:9; Matthew 7:21

The divinity of the Son
Colossians 2:9; Philippians 2:6; Titus 2:13

The divinity of the Holy Spirit
2 Corinthians 3:17; Judges 3:10; Job 33:4

Spend some time getting feedback, checking that the verses have been correctly identified, and talking through any problems.

Regulations

The Trinity is regulative. It is a guide against heresy. As God reveals himself to us, so he is.

Ask members if they have ever been visited by Jehovah's Witnesses. If they have, ask them to share what they experienced. Were they able to spot any misunderstanding of the Trinity? (JWs do not believe that Jesus is divine, but that he was the first of the created order; furthermore, they say the Spirit is not a person – it is just a force and so can't be God.) Explain that the Trinity is a good guide as to whether sects or cults are preaching orthodox Christianity.

Heresy-spotting

In a short input explain about these three possible mistakes. Use some dressing-up clothes and two members to help you.

SESSION 6

A) ACTOR GOD *(Modalism)*. One God in three different disguises. (Go off and get changed twice.) — dress up 3 Y/P.

B) BOSS GOD *(Subordinationism)*. One God with adopted son and subordinate Spirit. (Get two members to stand next to you. The first says to the second, 'You're more important than me.' The second says, 'Yes, but he's more important than both of us.')

C) COMPETING GODS *(Tritheism)*. Three Gods. (The three of you all argue, 'I'm God.' 'No, I'm God.' Etc.) — Get them to argue.

➤ DOING IT

Singing

This is probably the place for some of those simple songs that have three verses successively mentioning Father, Son and Holy Spirit, such as 'Father we love you'. Or how about singing the Doxology: 'Praise God from whom all blessings flow'? Or, if you can manage it, sing one of those fine hymns with a Trinitarian final verse, such as:

Holy, Holy, Holy,
Lord God Almighty!
Early in the morning
Our song shall rise to thee.

The Trinity is an old established doctrine, so celebrate with an old established song or two.

'To reflect upon God in his three-in-oneness, Father, Son, Spirit, in their distinguishable persons and functions yet perfect unity and harmony in mutual, everlasting love, is to catch a vision of something so unspeakably glorious, even beautiful and attractive, that it has ever and again down the centuries moved men and women to the heights of adoring worship, love and praise.' (Bruce Milne, *Know The Truth*, IVP)

Praying

Before praying together, discuss how members tend to pray. Perhaps we ought to pray, 'to the Father, through the Son, by the Holy Spirit.' Encourage Trinitarian thinking: 'Jesus in my heart, by the power of the Spirit, to the glory of God the Father.'

Koinonia

This is the Greek word for 'fellowship'. If God is three then at the heart of the Godhead is fellowship, relationship. As God is, so we can be. We only find out who we really are in relationships, families, groups – yes, even youth groups. Why not cement your fellowship tonight by sharing a sign of peace (kiss, hug, handshake), but offer it in a Trinitarian formula to each other:

'The peace of the Lord, the power of the Spirit and the love of the Father be always with you.'
2 Cor 13:14.

WORK-OUT

BELIEVE IT OR WHAT?

Grade your responses to the ten statements using the following scores:

5 strongly agree   **4** agree   **3** no opinion on this

2 disagree   **1** strongly disagree

1. I believe that the Bible clearly describes the Trinity. ✗
2. I believe that Jesus Christ is divine. God ✓
3. I believe that the Holy Spirit is divine. God ✓
4. I believe God is best understood as a Father. Happy to call God father.
5. Other faiths can teach me things about God. ✓
6. All religions lead to God. ✓
7. If a religion isn't Trinitarian it is seriously flawed. ✗
8. My youth leader's got great teeth. ✓
9. Jesus Christ is the greatest person who ever lived. ✓
10. I find the doctrine of the Trinity straightforward. ✓

Trinity is: A church in Long Eaton. A girl's name. God, Son + Holy Spirit. All three (one) are like.

VERSE SEARCH

	Three separate	Three one	Divine Father	Divine Son	Divine Spirit
Genesis 1:26	…………	…………	…………	…………	…………
Judges 3:10	…………	…………	…………	…………	…………
Job 33:4	…………	…………	…………	…………	…………
Matthew 6:9	…………	…………	…………	…………	…………
Matthew 7:21	…………	…………	…………	…………	…………
Matthew 28:19	…………	…………	…………	…………	…………
Mark 1:9-11	…………	…………	…………	…………	…………
John 10:30	…………	…………	…………	…………	…………
John 14:16-17a	…………	…………	…………	…………	…………
Acts 2:32-36	…………	…………	…………	…………	…………
2 Corinthians 3:17	…………	…………	…………	…………	…………
Galatians 1:1	…………	…………	…………	…………	…………
Philippians 2:6	…………	…………	…………	…………	…………
Colossians 2:9	…………	…………	…………	…………	…………
Titus 2:13	…………	…………	…………	…………	…………

EQUIPMENT CHECKLIST
(Depending on which sections you tackle, you may need)
- Several identical pieces of wood and a saw
- A flip-chart or piece of wallpaper
- Blow football set
- Clean table-tennis balls
- Sweets or chocolate biscuits
- List of words
- Copies of Work-out sheet
- Bibles
- Prepared packages as visual aids
- Encyclopaedia

SESSION 7: THE PERSON OF THE HOLY SPIRIT

Up Close and Personal

◆ TEACHING POINT
The Holy Spirit is the third person of the Trinity.

◆ GROUP AIM
To grasp that the Spirit can only be properly understood as a person, rather than as a thing.

LEADERS' GUIDE

The person of the Holy Spirit is another tricky doctrine to master. By the very nature of the Spirit, attention is always drawn to the Father and the Son. The Spirit is not self-seeking but exists to draw people into relationship with the other two members of the Trinity. Consequently, although wanting to understand the Spirit in terms of personality, we will find far more material concerning the work, rather than the person, of the Spirit.

We're aware that words like 'wind' and 'blow' have a high snigger potential. We've not gone wildly out of our way to avoid *double entendre* in this session, but you, mindful as you are of your group's capacity to giggle at almost anything on a bad night, may have to exercise sensitivity and restraint.

BIBLE BACKGROUND

The Hebrew word for Spirit is *ruah*. It also means 'wind'. However, it usually denotes God's activity in the world. For instance, in **Psalm 148:8**, the wind 'does his bidding'.

In the New Testament, the Greek word *pneuma* also means wind or breath. In **2 Timothy 3:16** we read that Scripture is 'God-breathed' (*theopneustos*). Almost literally, it has been 'God-spirited'.

In **John 14:16** we read that Jesus promises 'another Counsellor' from the Father. There are two Greek words for 'another'. *Heteros* means 'alternative' or 'different'. *Allos* means 'further' or 'additional'. Here it is *allos* that is used. The promised Holy Spirit is another counsellor of the same kind; additional and further support. Therefore the Spirit is person and personality just as much as Jesus the Son is.

The Greek noun is neuter (neither male nor female) yet the New Testament always calls the Spirit 'he' (**John 16:13**). We need not read too much into the use of a masculine pronoun. It is personhood that is being affirmed, not

SESSION 7

maleness. So we understand the Holy Spirit as the third person of the Trinity, but we are not affirming that the Spirit is a person exactly like we are. 'Person', here, is a technical term of theology.

In **Ephesians 4:30** we discover that it is possible to grieve the Holy Spirit of God. This would be a nonsense if the Spirit were an impersonal force, or in any sense neuter. The Holy Spirit is capable of grieving. Only a person can do this.

Throughout the New Testament, the key texts about the Spirit are either confessional (enabling truth about Son or Father to be stated) or doxological (giving glory to Son or Father). These come together in **1 Corinthians 12:3**.

In *Reflected Glory* (Hodder and Stoughton, 1975), Tom Smail points out that the best translation of 'indescribable gift' (**2 Corinthians 9:15**) is 'not-yet-fully-drawn-out gift'. God's fully-drawn-out gift to us is his Son – dead, risen and ascended. God's not-yet-fully-drawn-out gift is the Holy Spirit, who leads us into all the Son and the Father have for us.

➤ STARTING IT

Sawn off

Get hold of some pieces of wood. It doesn't matter what they look like, or how big they are, but they all need to be identical and you need enough for one between two in your group.

Take each piece of wood and saw it into two uneven pieces. Divide each piece differently. Write on one piece 'Holy Spirit' and on the other 'Father and Son'.

Place all the wood in the middle of the room and invite each member to take one piece. By co-operating they now need to find their partner. If you have cut the wood carefully it shouldn't be too easy to do this exercise like a jigsaw. Everyone will only know they are right when all the joined pieces are the same length. (Tip: to have an even number in your group, either join in, or don't.)

Explain, once finished, that the Holy Spirit only makes sense as part of the Trinity, belonging with, and drawing attention to, the other two members of it. Father, Son and Holy Spirit are a unity and lead into unity, not division (thus the co-operation part of the exercise). Read **Ephesians 4:3**.

Get each pair to write onto a flip-chart, or the blank side of a roll of wallpaper, a statement about the person of the Holy Spirit. If your group can cope with it, ask them to give biblical references to support their statement.

Breath games

In order to draw attention to the Spirit of God being described as the breath of God, spend a few opening minutes playing some breath games. See who can hold their breath the longest. Play blow-football. See who can blow a

SESSION 7

table-tennis ball the furthest out of their mouth. Or aim for a bucket and see who is most accurate.

Missing Spirit

Give out something nice, such as a chocolate biscuit or some sweets, to all but one or two members. (Choose victims who can cope.)

Read **Acts 19:1,2**. When Paul found a group of disciples who had missed out on the Holy Spirit he was surprised. Explain that the presence of the Holy Spirit in the life of a believer was so natural to the early Christians that it surprised them when someone had missed out. The Holy Spirit was so natural that they wrote little about the person of the Spirit (that must have been obvious) and lots about the work (which wasn't obvious and can still confuse Christians).

Give the goodies to those you overlooked.

➤ TEACHING IT

Word games

Make a list of words that are synonymous with the Holy Spirit.

Counsellor (**John 16:7**)	Spirit of truth (**John 14:17**)
Holy Ghost (Ancient English)	Spirit of Jesus (**Acts 16:7**)
Spirit of God (**Genesis 1:2**)	Spirit of the Lord (**Isaiah 61:1**)

Make another list of words that are descriptive of the Holy Spirit.

Dove (**Mark 1:10**) Wind (**Acts 2:2**) Fire (**Acts 2:3**)

We are still keeping clear of words that are descriptive of the Spirit's work, for that is the subject of the next session.

Ask members to fill in the words under the appropriate column of the Work-out sheet. Read some of the references for the more obscure titles.

Talky bit

Prepare five ordinary packages (such as empty cornflakes or soap powder boxes) by cutting along the edges so that they can be opened out flat. Write the following words (one per box) on an inside face of each package:

Personal	Special	Obedience
Spiritual	Eye-opening	

Close the boxes as neatly as possible. If you can make the joins undetectable that would be excellent.

Read **John 14:15-21**. In a short input make these points:

1. The Holy Spirit is the *personal* God, present with us (**verse 16**).
2. Jesus went physically, but sent a *spiritual* successor (**verses 16-18**).

SESSION 7

3. The Spirit is a *special* gift only for Christians; the world cannot accept or understand this (**verse 17**).
4. The Spirit *opens our eyes* to Jesus (**verses 19,20**).
5. *Obedience* is the attitude required to enable this to happen (**verses 15,21**).

As you get to each new point, ask a member to open up the box and reveal the hidden word.

Conclude that the Spirit is God's gift to ordinary people like you and me, just as you used ordinary, everyday things to illustrate your talk.

Who is it? Using an encyclopaedia, read out the biographies of some famous people. Get members to shout out as soon as they know who you are describing. Throw in a few popular musicians and sports stars for good measure.

Make the point that we identify people by what they do. Explain that in the next session you are going to be looking at the *work* of the Spirit but in this session you have been identifying *personality*.

If your group can cope with long words, explain that this session has been ontological (concerning the Spirit's being) but the next one will be functional (concerning the Spirit's doing).

➤ DOING IT

Spiritcreed Using the words on the Work-out sheet, recite the part of the Nicene Creed which refers to the Holy Spirit.

Memory verse 'I will ask the Father, and he will give you another Counsellor to be with you for ever – the Spirit of truth' (**John 14:16a**).

At this point, it's worth checking again that memory verses from previous sessions are still remembered.

Not-yet-fully-drawn-out Read out **2 Corinthians 9:15** and explain that next time you will be going on to describe that indescribable work.

Prayer End with a short prayer, perhaps using the grace. Get members to turn it up from **2 Corinthians 13:14** so they understand it is a biblical closing prayer.

WORK-OUT

WORD GAMES

synonymous	descriptive
------------	------------
------------	------------
------------	------------
------------	------------
------------	------------
------------	------------

SPIRITCREED

'We believe in the Holy Spirit,

the Lord, the giver of life,

who proceeds from the Father and the Son.

With the Father and the Son he is worshipped and glorified.

He has spoken through the prophets.'

MEMORY VERSE

'I will ask the Father, and he will give you another Counsellor
to be with you for ever – the Spirit of truth'

(John 14:16a).

EQUIPMENT CHECKLIST
(Depending on which sections you tackle, you may need)
- Cans of economy baked beans
- A plastic sheet
- Teaspoons
- Balloons
- Video clip of poor refereeing
- Copies of Work-out sheets
- Bibles
- Pens and paper

SESSION 8: THE WORK OF THE HOLY SPIRIT

Danger – Spirit at Work

◆ TEACHING POINT
To introduce the work of the Holy Spirit.

◆ GROUP AIM
To give the group realistic expectations of the work of the Spirit in their lives.

☞ **LEADERS' GUIDE**

Sometimes we can pray prayers such as this one:

'Lord, I'm going to spend the next few hours writing about the work of someone whose inspiration I'm beginning to doubt. Help!' (Can you imagine what sort of person prayed this prayer?)

The work of the Holy Spirit can be very difficult to observe. We can only see it from where we are and if, one particular day, we feel uninspired, it can be tempting to assume that the Holy Spirit is off working on a more important project than helping us to write/preach/train/lead, etc. So, it is essential to get to grips with the biblical material to remind us of the work of the Holy Spirit, who is in action even when we don't feel inspired.

In discussing the work of the Holy Spirit we sometimes stress that we need to balance the miraculous with the day-to-day. This is not strictly true. The same Spirit who inspired the biblical authors to painstakingly write down what we now have as our Scriptures also inspired miracles of healing. Young Christians need to be taught that the miraculous does occur and they should be encouraged to pray for it; they should also be shown that God works in the day-to-day and his Spirit can help them with their examinations, searches for a job, relationships with that difficult brother or sister and any number of 'routine' matters.

In fact, if members pray for God, by his Spirit, to help them get on with their parents, it is quite likely that he will offer the gift of patience and endurance rather than a miraculous transformation in parental personality. But then again, miracles do happen....

☞ **BIBLE BACKGROUND**

There are many possible references in this section. We have chosen only one example in each case.

The Holy Spirit works for God's purposes

- *Creation* The Spirit of God was at work in creation and inspired Elihu (the youngest of Job's comforters) to speak (**Job 33:4**).

SESSION 8

- *Salvation* The Spirit of God was at work in Jesus, enabling him to proclaim justice and lead his people (**Matthew 12:15-21**).

- *Revelation* The Spirit of God inspired the biblical writers to reveal God's truth to us (**Revelation 1:10,11**).

The Holy Spirit empowers God's people

- *Unity* Where the Spirit of the Lord is, there is unity (**Ephesians 4:3-6**).

- *Energy* Peter is energized to preach and heal (**Acts 2:1-7; 4:8-10**).

- *Guidance* Paul and his companions are aware of the Spirit opening and closing doors on their missionary journeys (**Acts 16:6-10**).

- *Calling* Ezekiel, the Old Testament prophet, identifies his calling with the work of the Spirit (**Ezekiel 2:1,2**).

- *Equipping* God's Spirit equipped Joseph to carry out the work of Pharaoh (**Genesis 41:37-40**).

- *Teaching* The Holy Spirit reminds us of Jesus' teaching (**John 14:26**).

The Holy Spirit leads individuals

- *Enables* a new start When the Holy Spirit indwells someone it is possible to have a new beginning, as if being born again (**John 3:5-7**).

- *Convicts* 'If God were our conscience we would all agree about right and wrong' (John White). But he isn't, and the Holy Spirit needs to prick our consciences regularly (**John 16:8-11**).

- *Protects* Believing Christians need not worry. Words will be given to us when necessary (**Matthew 10:19,20**) and the inheritance is secure (**Ephesians 1:13,14**).

- *Gives gifts* Don't assume that the various lists of gifts in the New Testament epistles are the only illustration of this. Look at the Spirit's gifting of Bezalel and colleagues (**Exodus 31:1-11**).

- *Transforms* The work of the Spirit is the transformation of the faithful, into the likeness of Christ (**2 Corinthians 3:18**).

- *Intercedes* How reassuring to know that our garbled prayers are acceptable to God because the Spirit is our go-between (**Romans 8:26,27**). This ties in with the work of Jesus as intercessor.

SESSION 8

➤ STARTING IT

Full of beans

✪ ✪

Place a plastic sheet in the middle of the room. Open a tin of economy (i.e. sloppy) baked beans and tip it onto the sheet. Invite members to use teaspoons to refill the can. (You can use two or more tins and do this as a race if you want. You need to be confident that a food fight will not develop, unless you really hate that wallpaper.)

Explain that we can tell what's inside a tin by what comes out if we spill it. Likewise humans, full of the Spirit, will react calmly and spiritually when bumped into, contents spilled, put under pressure, stretched, etc. If we are full of beans, beans will come out. If we are full of the Spirit....

The work of the Spirit fills us, to overflowing.

Balloons

✪ ✪

Link this session with the previous one by reminding members of the teaching about the Spirit as the breath of God (Hebrew: *ruah*; Greek: *pneuma*).

Point out that we get words like pneumatic (works by compressed air) and pneumonia (inflammation in the lungs) from the Greek word.

Hand out balloons. Does anyone know any tricks with them? The Holy Spirit is a bit like the difference between the balloon before and after inflation. The Holy Spirit is the breath of God, bringing us to life.

Spend a few minutes on balloon games. An oldie but goodie is to sit two teams facing each other about three metres apart. Without bums leaving seats they must try and bash the balloon over the back of the opposing line. A point is scored for doing this.

Bad refereeing

✪

Show a video clip of an appalling refereeing. Discuss the incident. Alternatively, have a game to begin with which you deliberately referee badly so that everyone argues with you.

When everyone has calmed down and you've had the stitches put in, discuss your performance. Make the point that everyone notices a bad referee, but nobody notices a good one. The Holy Spirit's entire work is to bring glory to Father and Son. It is not surprising that we don't notice the third person of the Trinity sometimes. It also reminds us to pay more attention to the place the Spirit directs us than to the one who does the directing.

➤ TEACHING IT

Profile

✪ ✪ ✪

Give out the Work-out sheets. Ask members, perhaps working with a partner, to look up a few references each and to piece together the Holy Spirit Work Profile which they can write onto the sheet. Share results.

SESSION 8

Spirit in me
✪ ✪

Get members to complete the questions on the Work-out sheet. Share results.

Read out these words from the song, 'Jesus, we celebrate Your Victory':

'His Spirit in us releases me from fear
The way to him is open, with boldness we draw near
And in his presence our problems disappear,
Our hearts responding to his love.'
(John Gibson, Thankyou Music)

Mention that we only see our problems in true perspective if we draw nearer to Jesus. It is in this sense that they 'disappear'.

Bible study
✪ ✪ ✪

For a group Bible study, look at **John 16:5-16**. Read the passage together and then discuss:

1. When someone says 'Holy Spirit' what do you think of? What image do you have in your mind? (Allow members to share from their imaginations.)

2. Is the Holy Spirit a person or a thing?
(Always described as 'he' not 'it', **verses 7, 8, 13, 14.**)

3. Why did Jesus say he had to go?
(In this passage, because the Holy Spirit could not come until he had gone, **verse 7**.)

4. Why is the coming of the Spirit not possible until Jesus has gone?
(Again, in this passage, because he is sent by Jesus, from where Jesus is going, **verse 7**. The Holy Spirit is without physical limitations and can work in 'the world' (**verse 8**) not just locally.)

What is the work of the Holy Spirit?
(Convicting the world (**verse 8**), guiding into truth (**verse 13**), speaking and telling (**verse 13**), bringing glory to God (**verse 14**).)

➤ DOING IT

Saatchi and Spirit
✪ ✪

An excellent slogan for the work of the Holy Spirit in the life of a believer is this:

If you do before you get it, what you would do if you had it, then you've got it.

Invite members, working in small groups if necessary, to draw attention to the work of the one who draws attention to Father and Son. How would they go about advertising the Holy Spirit so that others want more, or so that those not yet Christian want to be drawn in? Give out drawing materials and paper and give them a good chunk of time. Display the best results where others can see them.

WORK-OUT

Holy Spirit work profile – The work of the Holy Spirit is...

Job 33:4..

Matthew 12:15-21 ....

Revelation 1:10,11 ....

Ephesians 4:3-6...

Acts 2:1-7; 4:8-10..

Acts 16:6-10..

Ezekiel 2:1,2..

Genesis 41:37-40...

John 14:26 ....

John 16:8-11...

John 3:5-7...

Matthew 10:19,20 ....

Ephesians 1:13,14 ....

Exodus 31:1-11...

2 Corinthians 3:18 ....

Romans 8:26,27..

Spirit in me

If the spirit of Alan Shearer lived in me I would..

If the spirit of the Queen lived in me I would..

If the spirit of Tina Turner lived in me I would..

If the spirit of Nelson Mandela lived in me I would..

If the Spirit of Jesus lived in me I would..

EQUIPMENT CHECKLIST
(Depending on which sections you tackle, you may need)
- Lego or other children's building materials
- Baggy clothes, old rags and newspapers
- Four waste bins
- At least 12 tennis balls
- Dramatised Bible
- Copies of Work-out sheet and problem cards
- Cardboard and sticky tape
- Flip-chart and pens (or OHP and screen)
- Bibles
- Paper, freezer labels and string

SESSION 9: THE CHURCH AS BODY

Body Language

◆ TEACHING POINT
The church consists of people serving Christ in many ways according to the different gifts he has given.

◆ GROUP AIM
For the group to see the church in this way and for members to begin to explore how they might serve the church.

☞ LEADERS' GUIDE

'Biblical religion is inescapably corporate. Even before the fall Adam was not fulfilled without a human partner.' (Bruce Milne).

Your faith is a corporate activity. Being a Christian in Little Gidding, Lower Godney or even Left of Gateshead involves being part of the body there. Christianity cannot be isolationist. Once converted, Christians should expect a relationship with other Christians to follow. We are part of the local body and the catholic (world-wide) Church.

The skill of the youth leader is to grow a group with strong relationships and spiritual maturity, thus avoiding any tendency to be a clique.

☞ BIBLE BACKGROUND

The passage most famously pointed to when talking about the church as body is **1 Corinthians 12:12-31**. Every-member ministry within the church requires that each member has a part to play and the parts work together for the benefit of the whole. The gifts (all of them) are to build up the church. Headline, or 'up-front', gifts are no more important than behind-the-scenes gifts.

The church functions as a body in that diverse gifts are put together to make one, functioning whole. It is not that everyone thinks the same (that would make the church an automaton, not a body) but that Christ takes the variety of gifts, interests and personalities and brings them together to serve him (**Romans 12:4-8**).

Paul uses the image of the body in more than one way in his writings. In **1 Corinthians 6:15-17** he uses it to prohibit sexual immorality. Uniting with a prostitute (it is probably some sort of cultic prostitution that is being argued against here) whilst being part of the body of Christ is uniting immorality and grace. Not possible.

In Colossians, Paul writes about the relationship between the head and the rest of the body. The head of the body is not the minister, or the youth leader (as if), but Jesus Christ (**Colossians 1:18,24**). Losing connection with the head

PAGE 51

SESSION 9

is the worst possible thing for a body, obviously (**Colossians 2:19**). The peace of Christ, the head, should rule in the heart of the body (**Colossians 3:15**).

In **Romans 12:5** and **1 Corinthians 10:16** Paul shows us that Christ is the whole body and we are members of it. This analogy reminds us that Christ is Lord of all the parts of the whole body. We are his. We're not just ruled by him, but are to see ourselves as a part of him.

Romans 15:5-7 stresses the fundamental unity there ought to be within the body if it is to be 'one'. It needs one heart and one mouth. The parts of the body need to be accepting of each other. There is additional material in Ephesians, which is primarily about the church. We have majored here on other passages.

➤ STARTING IT

Same difference

Play this game by taking it in turns to make statements which begin either:

'We're all the same because...' or 'We're all different because...'

The secret of making an 'acceptable' statement is this: if someone says, 'We're all the same...' they must state something which begins with the first letter of their Christian name. So, Simon would say, 'We're all the same because we all have secrets.' If we want to say, 'We're all different', we must talk about something that begins with the next letter of the alphabet. 'We're all different because we all wear different trainers' or 'We all live in different towns,' says Simon.

Keep going until most people have got it. You may want to brief a few members before the session so more than one person is in the know to start with. Conclude that the church consists of varied gifts (we're all different) serving one purpose (we're all the same). Clever, eh?

Corporate

Make two identical, simple models out of Lego or other toy building materials. Break one up and give one or more pieces of it to each member of the group. Put the other one behind a screen. Members take it in turns to go and look at the model and then assemble their piece into the whole. No discussion. No conferring. No touching each other's pieces. Talk about co-operation and each playing their part.

Body building

Have available some baggy clothes and newspaper and old rags to stuff into them. The aim is to make two volunteers into hunks by stuffing the rags and newspapers in. Then the two models can have a posing competition for a while.

SESSION 9

Contrived link: 'Body building is not just about muscles. We are all part of another body.'

Binball
✪ ✪

For this game you need four waste bins, a minimum of four players (with stamina) and twelve tennis balls. Place the bins in the four corners of the room, or spaced a few metres apart outdoors. Place the tennis balls in a pile in the middle, equidistant from all four bins.

Each contestant owns a bin and stands by it. The bin may not be moved. The aim is to get four balls, one at a time, back to your bin. On the command 'go' each contestant runs to the pile of balls and takes one back to their bin. When the pile in the centre is finished they can take balls from other contestant's bins.

If you want to make it a more strategic game play in pairs, threes or fours. If you want it to last longer then increase the number of balls and / or the amount required to win. It is a very tiring and frustrating game. Playing with a colleague makes it easier. Conclude that the church should be a place of co-operation not competition.

➤ TEACHING IT

Key passage
✪ ✪ ✪

Read 1 Corinthians 12:12-27
The Dramatised Bible (Marshall Pickering) has a version which is worth checking out.

Having read it, give members, working in groups if necessary, a note of the other passages where gifts are mentioned: **Romans 12:3-8; Ephesians 4:7-13; 1 Peter 4:7-11**.

Ask them to write onto a flip-chart, or large piece of paper, all the gifts that are spoken of. Which are duplicated? Which are unique to one passage?

Strength or advantage
✪ ✪

Take the list on the Work-out sheet and ask members, working alone, to decide if the mentioned item is a strength or an advantage.

Gifts are given by God to build up his church. A natural talent, or strength, becomes a gift when it is offered in God's service. You don't find 'musicianship' in any of the New Testament gifts lists, but there can be no doubt that it is a talent which can be used to serve the church. It is therefore a strength, not an advantage.

Advantages are the result of living in a world to which God has given freedom. This can seem unfair, but an advantage can be used to serve God. For instance, someone with a nice house (advantage) can use it to host meetings for the church, or can exercise the gift of hospitality. An advantage can enable you to exercise a particular gift. A salesperson will say that an

SESSION 9

advantage can make you the contact, but you need the gift to get the contact to become a customer.

Here is our suggested list of answers:

1. Strength	6. Strength	11. Strength	16. Strength
2. Advantage	7. Strength	12. Strength	17. Strength
3. Advantage	8. Advantage	13. Advantage	18. Strength
4. Advantage	9. Strength	14. Strength	19. Strength
5. Strength	10. Strength	15. Strength	20. Advantage

There may need to be some discussion as you may not (gasp!) all agree with each other.

Limited building

Provide the group with a large amount of cardboard and a roll of sticky tape. The task is to build a chair, capable of holding you, the leader. However, they must first read the limitation on the card you give them, photocopied from the Work-out sheet.

Make the point that working together is necessary for the church to achieve its purpose.

➤ DOING IT

What do I do?

Brainstorm all the different things members of your group do within the church at the moment. Go on to talk about areas of further service they would like to investigate. Make sure they realize that their school work and family should take priority on their time.

Faces in the crowd

On a large piece of paper get members to draw themselves in a huge crowd, like the audience at a gig. Then place labels (freezer labels are good) round the edge of the picture and on each label write down the person's main gifts (help each other if members are being modest) and use the string to join the label to the person.

Make the point that we are more than faces in the crowd. We are unique and special in the sight of God and we have gifts and skills that are needed by the church.

Memory verse

1 Corinthians 12:14 'Now the body is not made up of one part but of many.'

PAGE 54

WORK-OUT

STRENGTH OR ADVANTAGE?

1. I'm courteous.	....	11. I'm good at maths.	....
2. I have lots of friends.	....	12. I can read aloud confidently.	....
3. I have a lovely home.	....	13. I have ten GCSEs.	....
4. My parents are wealthy.	....	14. I'm well organized.	....
5. I can cook.	....	15. I'm a good judge of character.	....
6. I can play netball.	....	16. I have imagination.	....
7. I can drive.	....	17. I can run a marathon.	....
8. I have a new car.	....	18. I can tell others about Jesus.	....
9. I'm encouraging.	....	19. I know New-Testament Greek.	....
10. I can explain things.	....	20. I have a guitar.	....

Working together – Problem cards

You have broken both your legs and can't move from your seat.	**You have lost the ability to speak; you can only listen.**
You have broken both your wrists and can't touch anything.	**You are to be blindfolded and cannot see.**

EQUIPMENT CHECKLIST
(Depending on which sections you tackle, you may need)

- Play-doh™
- Flip-chart or OHP
- Jobs on cards
- People from the church
- Verses on cards
- Bibles
- Things to weigh and a set of balance scales
- Copies of Work-out sheet

SESSION 10: THE CHURCH AS FELLOWSHIP

Getting Churched

◆ TEACHING POINT
The main functions of the church are worship and mission.

◆ GROUP AIM
That the group should begin to behave as a part of the church, local and world-wide.

☞ **LEADERS' GUIDE**

The previous session could have been a bit inward-looking. But the main task of the church is worship, and to bring others to a relationship with God so that they want to worship too. It's been said before, but the church exists for the benefit of its non-members. Members worship and communicate their desire to worship to others. That is the gist of evangelism. One summary would be that worship is when the church is 'in' and mission is when it is 'out'.

So, is your youth fellowship a church? We'll try and answer that question, but a more important one is, 'Do the members understand what it is to be part of the worshipping community?'

☞ **BIBLE BACKGROUND**

The Greek word *koinonia* describes a 'sharing together in something'. Let's piece together the material that tells us about the koinonia of the church.

In **Exodus 16:23-30** God stipulates that the Sabbath is to be a day of rest. In the fourth commandment (**Exodus 20:8**) it becomes a day of worship too. Early Christian koinonia was built around the synagogue on the seventh day of the week. As Christian worship moved out of the synagogue the day also changed to the first day of the week, the day the resurrection was celebrated (**Acts 20:7**). Koinonia is a sharing together in worship.

Luke 9:46-50 tells us that the church can expect (these actions and stories are enacted parables) to include all who serve Jesus. It is not a place for bragging about superiority (**verse 46**). It includes children (**verses 47,48**). It includes those expected to be outsiders (**verse 50**). Koinonia comes from having in common the Lordship of Christ.

John 10:14-18 reminds us that the church is not a group without order or shape but consists of believers known to Jesus by name. There may be other churches (denominations) but distinction and identity serves Christ's unique mission as long as all remain in fellowship with his wider family. Koinonia people have unity and diversity.

John 17:11 reminds us, as we saw in the session on Jesus' ascension, that he

SESSION 10

continues to care for his church and intercede on its behalf. The unity of the church is personality-based not organizationally-based. Jesus and the Father are united in love and purpose; so the church must be.

Acts 2:42-47 shows us the early church community in action. The total experience of teaching, fellowship, bread-breaking and prayer led to church growth.

Put these passages together and you get a church which ministers; first to its members (**Galatians 6:10**) and then to the world by being salt and light (**Matthew 5:16**).

It follows that if a church seeks unity in Christ so should a youth group. Your church, and your group should have no grudges or resentments but be places where members are accepted for themselves (**Romans 15:7**). The essential expression of koinonia is agape love. This is usually translated simply as 'love' but our English word is insufficiently sturdy to cope with all the implications of an agape commitment. **1 John 3:16** and **4:10** set out Jesus' love for, and commitment to, his people as the pattern of our love for each other.

1 Corinthians 13 tells us that demonstrating agape love is the 'most excellent way' for a fellowship. It is also a rebuke against practices within worship that exclude outsiders. **1 Corinthians 13** should not be read out of context. **1 Corinthians 14:39** reminds us that Paul has been writing in order to encourage the church's worship to be fitting and orderly.

Romans 5:5 tells us clearly that love is a gift of the Spirit.

The four key English words to describe the function of the church are:

      WORSHIP   FELLOWSHIP   MINISTRY   WITNESS

➤ STARTING IT

Worship
✪ ✪

Since the main point of this session is that the church is here to worship God, why not start with an imaginative time of worship and praise? Use singing or some instrumental music and words from the Psalms. Why not invite members to worship God creatively by drawing, or making a model out of Play-doh™ whilst this is happening?

What for?
✪ ✪ ✪

Ask the question, 'What is the church for?' Write up all the answers on a flip-chart, OHP or large piece of paper as members shout them out.

Jobsworth
✪

Or start with the jobs. Make a list of all the jobs that need doing in a church. It would be impressive if you could also name the people who do them, but if you can't, ask members to research and report back. A different way to achieve the same end would be to start with some prepared, old index cards and write on each a job that exists in the church. Members have to

SESSION 10

write on the back of the card the name of the person who does each job. Advanced planners may like to invite some lesser-known saints along to the meeting and ask members to guess which jobs they do. If you had ten guests and ten jobs to be matched to the right person it could be fun. Ask each of them how their task furthers worship or mission.

➤ TEACHING IT

Church verses
✪ ✪ ✪

Write on cards some verses from the Bible background material. Working in small groups if necessary, ask members to search for the verses and report on what they add to our understanding of the church's function.

Weigh hey hey
✪ ✪

Here's a problem, suitable for mathematically unchallenged groups.

You have twelve snooker balls. They look identical. However, one is a different weight from the other eleven. You don't know which one it is and you don't know if it's heavier or lighter. Fortunately you have an old-fashioned set of balance scales. Can you find the dodgy ball and say if it's heavier or lighter than the rest, in three weighings?

This exercise is quite a complicated matter of reason and logic. Encourage your group to work together, or in smaller groups, to solve it. A hint would be to tell them to be sure to record every bit of information they learn at each weighing. Equipment is unnecessary, but if you can offer members the chance actually to do the experiment with a balance and twelve identical-looking things one of which is a slightly different weight, that would be acey-pacey (well, good anyway). The solution is on page 61.

Read **Acts 2:44** and explain to the group that a fellowship is a place where members have, '...everything in common'. Churches and fellowships are to be places of togetherness and co-operation, not cliquiness and individuality. If a member of a fellowship faces a problem, then all the members face it. If you want to lead on to a discussion where there may be some disagreement, suggest a debate with the motion, 'This house believes that it is unnecessary for every member of a church to own a lawnmower and a ladder.' You could choose some culturally relevant wording for your lot.

Furthermore, linking to the next items if you are doing them, the church needs to be a place of balance. Extremism often leads a group of Christians to focus on one task of the church, to the detriment of the whole fellowship. Pointing all tasks in the general direction of worship or mission will help balance a fellowship.

How does it help?
✪ ✪

How does each separate task within the fellowship of the church link with evangelism or worship? Consider this by asking the question, 'What would the church be like if this job wasn't done?' Here's some examples:

PAGE 58

SESSION 10

If nobody counted the offering....   If nobody made coffee after worship....
If nobody cleaned the drains....   If nobody taught the under-sevens....

If you come across any jobs that don't seem to contribute anything to the church's worship or evangelism then why not write, as a group, to the church leaders and suggest the job is unnecessary.

Four corners ✪

This is an exercise for groups that have more than about twelve members, for they need to divide into four and move into the four corners of the meeting room. You can do the exercise as one group but it will take longer. Each group is invited to make the case that the church should concentrate on one of the following:

WORSHIP   FELLOWSHIP   MINISTRY   WITNESS

Groups should justify their position with Bible verses if possible. Some churches spend time concentrating on these things in cycles. They end up chasing the mistake. For instance, whilst improving worship they lose sight of the need for ministry or witness. Discuss which of the four corners best represents your own church's focus at the moment.

Are we or aren't we? ✪ ✪

Ask members to consider the question, 'Is our group a church?' You may like to divide a large piece of paper in half with these headings:

WE ARE BECAUSE...   WE AREN'T BECAUSE...

The New Testament knows nothing of a church with limitations caused by gender, nationality, cultural background, height, musical preferences or age. Explain this, and read **Galatians 3:28**.

➤ DOING IT

Mission statement ✪ ✪ ✪

Work with the members on a mission statement for the group. It needs to be concise and to begin with the phrase, 'This group exists to....' There is a sample Mission Statement on the Work-out sheet that you might wish to photocopy.

Get smart ✪

Starting with the brainstormed list of what the church is for, aim to come up with some goals for the group over the next few months. Make sure they are SMART – that is:

Specific   **M**easurable   **A**chievable   **R**eviewable   **T**imed

Encourage goals that will build up the local church, not just the group.

Ministry ✪ ✪

Encourage members to pray for each other and to share needs for prayer or practical help.

PAGE 59

WORK-OUT

MISSION STATEMENT

This group exists to...

Our SMART goals are...

Puzzle solution

Weighing A

Discard balls 1, 2, 3, 4 and weigh 5, 6, 7, 8 against 9, 10, 11, 12. You will then know that the ball is either amongst 1 - 4, or 5 - 12. If it is among 5 - 12 you will be able to say whether it will prove to be light or heavy.

Let's say 5 - 8 goes down and 9 - 12 goes up.

Weighing B

You now know that if the defective ball is among 5 - 8 it will be heavy; if 9 -12 it will be light.

Discard 8, 11 and 12. Swap 5 and 6 with 9. Add 1, 2 and 3 which you can use as standard. Weigh 1, 3, 7, 9 against 2, 5, 6, 10.

If 1, 3, 7, 9 goes down then either 7 is heavy or 10 is light. (Weighing C) weigh one of them against 1, 2, 3 or 4.

If 2, 5, 6, 10 goes down then either 5 or 6 is heavy, or 9 is light. Discard 9 and (Weighing C) weigh 5 against 6. If one goes down, it is the heavy ball. If they balance then 9 is light.

If Weighing B balances exactly then the 'bad' ball is either a heavy 8 or a light 11 or 12. Discard 8 and (Weighing C) weigh 11 against 12. If there's any movement then the side that goes up is the light ball. If they balance then 8 is heavy.

If at Weighing A the two pans balance then 1, 2, 3 or 4 is the defective ball. Discard 4 and (Weighing B) weigh 1 and 2 against 3 and (say) 10.

If 1 and 2 go down then either 1 or 2 is heavy or 3 is light. Discard 3 and (Weighing C) weigh 1 against 2. The side that goes down is the heavy ball; if no movement then 3 is light.

If 3 and 10 go down then either 1 or 2 is light, or 3 is heavy. (Weighing C) Weigh 1 against 2. The side that goes up is the light ball, or, if they balance, then 3 is heavy.

If 1 and 2 balance with 3 and 10, then 4 is the defective ball. (Weighing C) Weigh it against any other ball to find out what is wrong with it.

QED

CYFA (14-18 year-olds) and **Pathfinders** (11-14s) are organizations which, as part of the Church Pastoral Aid Society, support the youth work of local churches throughout the UK.

Help is offered to local leaders through training (including annual events for full-time and voluntary leaders), members' events, Bible teaching resources, Ventures (great holidays with Christian teaching) and regular mailings for member groups.

CPAS is an evangelical, home missionary society which exists to strengthen Anglican churches to evangelize, teach and pastor people of all ages.

For under-11s **CPAS** has **Explorers, Climbers** and **Scramblers**.

CHURCH PASTORAL AID SOCIETY
Athena Drive, Tachbrook Park, WARWICK CV34 6NG

Tel: (01926) 334242
Fax: (01926) 337613

Email: ycd@cpas.org.uk
Internet: http://www.cpas.org.uk

COVIES

- **Covies** is an evangelical organization, 'Resourcing The Local Church' in its work with children and young people by helping them to attract and hold, lead to faith in Christ and equip for service as full members of the church.

- **Covies** helps churches by offering an age structure covering 0-20 years, providing training, support and resources for leaders, and events and evangelism opportunities for group members.

- The **Covies** package is Bible-based, church-controlled, inter-denominational, non-uniformed and flexible.

COVENANTERS
11-13 Lower Hillgate, STOCKPORT SK1 1JQ

Tel: (0161) 474 1262
Fax: (0161) 474 1300

Email: covies@dial.pipex.com

Other Resources from CPAS / Covies

Books that should be indispensable in a youth leader's library are:

CPAS Code

03428	Young People and the Bible	Phil Moon (Marshalls, 1993)
03591	Christian Youth Work	Phil Moon and Mark Ashton (Monarch, 1995)

Other books in the same series as *You'd Better Believe This Too!*

C16127	All Together Forever	Ephesians
C16129	Pressure Points	Issues that concern teenagers
C16130	Harping On?	Six Psalms
C16132	Repeat Prescription	The Ten Commandments
C16131	You'd Better Believe It!	Christian doctrine
C16134	Powered Up	Key moments from Acts
C16135	Just About Coping	Issues that teenagers have to cope with
C16136	Mission in Action	Broadening your group's horizons
C16137	People with a Purpose	Ten Old Testament characters
C16139	Outlawed by Grace	Galatians
C16138	Didn't He Used To Be Dead?	Jesus
C16141	Another Brick in the Wall	Nehemiah

Books from CPAS to resource your meetings:

C16128	Know Ideas!	Ideas to put into your programme
C16140	Know Ideas! 2	And some more...
C16133	Rave On	Ideas and principles for worship
C20010	DIY Worship	A bumper package of worship resources – including CD-rom
C18006	The ART of 14-18s	Age-range tools for leading groups

Books from Covies:

Focus on Relationships	
Focus on Practical Discipleship	
What's The Score?	A useful short evangelistic book with a football theme

CHURCH PASTORAL AID SOCIETY
Athena Drive, Tachbrook Park, WARWICK CV34 6NG
Tel: (01926) 334242   24-hour Sales Ansaphone: (01926) 335855

COVENANTERS
11/13, Lower Hillgate, STOCKPORT SK1 1JQ
Tel: (0161) 474 1262